ANCIENT MALTA

A Study of Its Antiquities

Harrison L_

illustrated by
Hilda Bruhm Lewis

Colin Smythe
Gerrards Cross, Bucks
1977

First published in 1977
by Colin Smythe Ltd.
Gerrards Cross, Bucks,
England

Cover picture: Bingemma catacombs

Photoset and Printed in Malta by Interprint (Malta) Ltd.

CONTENTS

ILLUSTRATIONS

ACKNOWLEDGEMENTS

I am obligated and grateful for the assistance received from authorities and experts of many kinds, as well as their written works, which has made possible a fabric from innumerable observations of details, to present a general description of the existing antiquities of Malta and through them a representation of the life and activities of ancient man on these Islands. If this account should contribute to a better understanding and appreciation of the magnificent archaeological heritage of Malta, it is to them that thanks are due.

Among those who have assisted particularly are Dr. David H. Trump, Professor of Archaeology at Cambridge University; Dott. Pasquale Testini, Professor of Archaeology at the University of Rome Institute of Christian Archaeology; Professor Michelangelo Cagiano de Azevedo, Universita del Sacro Cuore, Milan, and Missione Archeologica Italiana a Malta, Consiglio Nazionale Delle Ricerche, Rome; H. E. Mr. Itzhak Benyacov, Ambassador of Israel to Malta; Mr. Francis X. Mallia, Director of Museums Dept., Malta; Mr. T. C. Gouder, Archaeological Curator of the National Museum of Malta; Rev. Can. Dean A. Zammit Gabaretta, Assistant Librarian, Malta; Mgr. Rev. Vincent Borg, Professor of Christian Archaeology at the Royal University of Malta; Fr. Victor Camilleri, formerly in charge of the catacombs at St. Agatha's Church; and Fr. John Azzopardi, Curator of the Cathedral Museum, Mdina, Malta.

PREFACE

"For walk where we will, we tread upon some story". This was said by Cicero of Rome in the first century B.C., but even more remarkable it can also be said of Malta: and still today come upon some remainder of the ingenuity of ancient man. Few places in the world can offer such a great volume of more kinds of anti-quities than are concentrated in these two Islands. Beginning in 5000 B.C. and continuing down through almost 6,000 years, there were seven distinct ages of man on Malta, which are known solely or almost solely through observing and understanding the innumerable kinds of structures and handiworks remain-ing from each age.

The object of this study is to set forth in detail the best examples of the most representative types of antiquities of each age, placed, wherever possible, in chronological sequence, and to describe authentically as possible, the life and activities of ancient man during each of them.

The Neolithic, the Copper Age and the Bronze Ages have been identified and described by leading archaeologists since the first part of this century, and in recent years, they have been able to classify them precisely, according to each age. It is only with respect to the origin of the Middle Bronze Age people and of the cart-ruts identified with them, that an attempt has been made in this study to add to this knowledge.

An understanding of the Phoenician/Punic Age in Malta was extensively developed through excavations during 1963–70 by the Missione Archeologica Italiana a Malta, and through the study of their findings, a further analysis of this period has been possible.

With respect to the period of Roman occupation of Malta, a reassessment has been undertaken in view of the sparce and sometimes misleading conclusions of classical scholars, and the limited and uncorrelated investigation which had been made of the antiquities remaining from both the Republic and Imperial periods.

The exposition of the transition from Neo-Punic religious beliefs to the emergence of Christianity and its subsequent development during the first centuries is based for the most part on a detailed study of the catacombs. They reveal much that is significant to an understanding of this most important heritage of these Islands.

CHRONOLOGICAL TABLE

AGES OF ANCIENT MAN ON MALTA (By periods and phases)		ANTIQUITIES (Periods of those described in chapter)							
		II	III	IV	V	VI	VII	VIII	IX
NEOLITHIC[1]									
Ghar Dalam	5000 B.C.	*							
Grey Skorba	4700 B.C.	*							
Red Skorba	4400 B.C.	*							
COPPER AGE[1]									
Zebbug	4000 B.C.	*	*			*			
Mgarr	3600 B.C.	*	*			*			
Ggantija	3500 B.C.	*	*			*			
Saflieni	3000 B.C.	*	*			*			
Tarxien	2900 B.C.	*	*			*			
BRONZE AGES[1]									
Early	2400 B.C.	*		*					
Middle	1500 B.C.	*		*					
Late	1000 B.C.			*					
PHOENICIAN–PUNIC[1]									
Phoenician	850 B.C.					*	*		
Punic	600 B.C.					*	*	*	
ROMAN	218 B.C.				*		*	*	*
EARLY CHRISTIAN	60 A.D.								*

[1] Dates of periods supplied by Dr. D. H. Trump.

CHAPTER I

INTRODUCTION

Anicent Malta has become known primarily through the study of its antiquities; the development of the islands down through the ages seems best told, therefore, through placing the emphasis on the antiquities and man's relation to them rather than vice versa. Each of the main types of antiquities, in fact, symbolizes a particular age, and accordingly they are described here in chronological order following a brief introduction to the age in question. The antiquities of Malta which are identified with more than one age, such as the cave dwellings originally identified with the Neolithics, were either of less importance to other ages or were not especially significant for any one age alone.

The cave dwellings, which symbolize the Neolithic Period from 5000 to 4000 B.C., were sought out by these first inhabitants of Malta and Gozo, but in due course they built villages of rubble huts, as did other prehistoric peoples who lived initially in cave dwellings thereafter.

The magnificent megalithic temples were built by the Copper Age people who followed the Neolithics and lived on the islands for a millenium and a half until they disappeared suddenly and entirely except for a small remnant that later lost its identity.

The defence walls found on many of the ridges and plateaux were common to all Bronze Age inhabitants from about 2300 B.C. onward, while the dolmens are identified with only the Early Bronze Age and the silos and cart-ruts are thought to date particularly from the Middle and Late Bronze Ages.

The first sanctuary was established by the Phoenicians who founded trading centres in Malta and Gozo in 850 B.C.; it was further developed by the Carthaginians who occupied the islands in 600 B.C. and later established one or two other sanctuaries as well. The sanctuaries were developed and maintained by the native population, together with the Romans, who occupied the island in 218 B.C., until they became abandoned gradually during the I century A.D., due probably first to the concentration of the population in Melita and Gaulus respectively and the establishment of Roman temples.

9

The tombs to be found throughout Malta and Gozo are identified first with the Copper Age, while during the long centuries of the Bronze Age they cremated their dead, and then with the Phoenician–Punic Period, when they were located, almost exclusively in Malta. Through the artifacts found in them, much of the habits and activities of both the peoples of the Copper Age and the Phoenician–Punic Period has been determined.

The country estates, some of which date from the Punic period, were developed mostly during the Roman Republic era in the first two centuries B.C. Some were owned by the Romans, but generally they were occupied and maintained by the native Maltese who had emerged as a cultural variant and come to dominate the general life of the Islands by the time they were occupied by the Romans.

The walled cities of Melita and Gaulus, the defence towers, and the ports and stone paved roads built by the Romans best represent the life of the Islands under the Romans during the first two centuries of the Imperial Period.

The catacombs were developed mostly through the extension of Punic tombs, beginning with the transition from Neo-Punic beliefs in the I century up to the flowering of Christianity in the latter part of the II. Thereafter, they were developed extensively by the Christians during the III and IV centuries, and continued to be used up to the VII and possibly in the VIII century. Christian chapels were placed in their houses and within or beside their catacombs, while shrines outside the catacombs were developed during the III century and the Church appears to have claimed the site of St. Paul Milqi, where it is believed that St. Paul healed the sick, and made it into a shrine at the end of the IV century. A basilica was developed in St. Paul's Catacombs during the IV century and one was constructed independently of the catacombs at the former sanctuary of Tas-Silg at the end of the IV or beginning of the V century, while one was placed later in front of the Tad-Dejr Catacombs.

CHAPTER II

CAVE DWELLINGS, HUTS AND GIRNAS

The many natural caves of Malta and Gozo afforded ready homes for the first inhabitants who came to the islands in about 5000 B.C. They were Neolithics whose tools and implements were of stone, but they were well advanced in growing crops and in animal husbandry. They had come from Sicily but originally they stemmed from the East Mediterranean, i.e., Northern Syria and the South of Anatolia.[1] They brought with them in their small boats their domestic animals (goats, sheep, cattle, pigs), chattels and seeds (club wheat, barley, lentils)[2] prepared to cultivate the fertile fields of the two islands.

The caves they sought out in which they could also shelter their livestock and stores of goods, were selected apparently from the aspect of security from the wild animals, and were therefore located in the less accessible sides of cliffs and hills, while their fields were in the valleys often some distance from them. A few of the caves which were occupied by these original inhabitants have been identified. The first, which contained pottery associated with these people, was Ghar Dalam (575658)[3]. in Malta, which gave its name to this earliest phase. Their pottery has also been found in caves in Gozo; the most noteworthy is a series of about 20 caves strung around the ledge above Ghajn Abdul (287897).[3] Also, it appears that the half dozen or more caves in the cliff below Santa Verna (338895),[3] where their pottery was discovered underneath the ruins of the temple there, were probably occupied by them. The number and size of these two groups of caves appear to have attracted a relatively large proportion of the Neolithic population.

In addition to their crops, these cave dwellers no doubt produced a quantity of wool and possibly a rough woollen cloth which they could export in return for flint from Sicily and obsidian from the islands of Lipari and Pantelleria.

[1] L. Bernabo Brea, "Sicily", 1966, p. 38 (hereafter, Brea, 1966).

[2] D. H. Trump, "Malta: An Archaeological Guide", 1972, p. 20 (hereafter, Trump, 1972).

[3] Numbers indicate grid location on Malta and Gozo Survey map.

11

After some three hundred years, a development took place in their pottery; between 4700 and 4400 B.C., a new type called Grey Skorba, and locally derived out of Ghar Dalam pottery, was used, and again after three hundred years, another type called Red Skorba, came into use during 4400 to 4000 B.C.[4] The latter was derived from the Grey Skorba and from a Sicilian and Lipari ware, known as Diana. Both of these appear to have been developed locally and there is no evidence that Red Skorba ware was introduced into Malta by a new people from outside the islands.[5]

In due course, Neolithic man began to build huts to house him; evidence of these has been found beneath the temples at Skorba and, from the presence of their pottery found under the ruins of the Copper Age temples at Ta Hagrat in Mgarr in Malta and Santa Verna and Xewkija in Gozo, there may have been huts built by them there. These huts continued to be occupied during the temple period as well and the Early and Middle Bronze age people also had a village of huts at Borg in-Nadur, but the caves of both Malta and Gozo were used as dwellings through all the ages and even up to modern times.

Whether the corbel vault hut was used by the Neolithics and other prehistoric men in Malta is not known, although it appears that such a structure was used by them in Sardinia. But certainly these remarkable huts, which appear in many rural districts of Malta today, have been built and used as sheds if not as dwellings since very early times.

CAVE DWELLINGS

The caves of Malta and Gozo are among the most interesting natural features of these islands. Many show signs of having been inhabited by man down through the ages and many are still used by farmers as sheds or have built their houses into them. There are hundreds of caves on both islands and many of them are large to very large, some extending far into the interior of the hills where they are located.

As might be expected, the caves which have been used as dwellings open out in the cliffs above ravines or along the coasts which are bordered by high cliffs. Some are found in the sides of hills and a number are of karstic origin where the soft limestone has been washed away by underground streams and the rock surface has partially fallen in.

Most of them are easy to approach and enter and those described here, except where mentioned specifically, belong to this category. However, many of those that open out in the sides of cliffs high above the sea offer a challenge to even

[4] Trump, Skorba, 1966, pp. 24, 30, (hereafter, Trump 1966).
[5] J. D. Evans, "Malta in Antiquity" in the Blue Guide—Malta, p. 11.

the most skilled mountaineers, equipped with their ropes and all the paraphernalia required for that fascinating sport of the most intrepid.

Ghar Dalam

This cave, called in Maltese the dark cave, is the best known in Malta, not because of the fact that man on Malta first lived there but because of the bones deposited on its floor of extinct animals of the Pliestocene Age, some 250,000 years ago.[6] The Ghar Dalam Museum (575658) is on the right side of the road going down to Birzebbuga. It contains models of dwarf elephants and deer brought from elsewhere but the large number of other bones on display were found in the cave. A path leads down from the museum to the side of Wied Dalam and around to the entrance of the cave half way down.

The cave is interesting from the prehistoric point of view because the sherds found there afforded an insight into the inhabitation of the Maltese Islands from the earliest Neolithic period down to historical times and included not only those of the Ghar Dalam phase and the Grey Skorba phase which followed, but also all the phases of the Copper Age including the Zebbug, Mgarr, Ggantija and Tarxien, and all the Bronze Age phases.

Ghar Dalam had been used as a cow shed until its possible archaeological significance was noticed in 1865 and the first excavations were made. Not until 1892 was it excavated further but this was continued intermittently thereafter until 1934–37 when two levels containing pottery were identified.[7] One contained Punic to recent, and below it was one containing sherds of all the prehistoric phases. The maximum depth of both these levels was between 2' to $2\frac{1}{2}'$.[8]

Personal ornaments, tools and weapons as well as pottery and sherds, gave evidence that the cave had been used as a dwelling in Neolithic times and thereafter; the most remarkable were two plastic animal heads (figure 1), which were beautifully executed during the Ghar Dalam phase. They are on display at the National Museum. With a floor space of about 40 × 50 feet and 12' to 17' high, which is what

1. Ghar Dalam Plastic Animal Heads

one now sees upon entering, Ghar Dalam must have been quite commodius.

[6] Trump, 1972, p. 80.

[7] A. G. Agius, "Ghar Dalam Cave", 1970, pp. 15–17.

[8] J. D. Evans, "The Prehistoric Antiquities of the Maltese Islands", 1971, p. 19 (hereafter, Evans, 1971).

13

The cave appears originally to have receded into both sides from below the channel of the ravine, above which there appears to have been a funnel through which the torrent could rush, bringing the bones of the extinct animals with it. The recess in the side of the ravine, opposite to that of Ghar Dalam, has apparently been covered over with a bank of stones. Following the period when the bones were washed into the cave, the channel of the ravine was worn down leaving the cave high and dry some 50 feet or more above the bottom of the present channel.

Beyond the entrance, Ghar Dalam winds back where the bones were deposited in recesses of 3' to 5' or more and several feet in depth, and here and there are still traces of them. The wide path above the channel of the cave narrows after some 265 feet and divides into several channels. These probably continue on down to the Bay of St. George below and were once explored for a further 450 feet. For potholers, these depths may still offer an enticing opportunity for adventure.

Cave of the Bats

Going on down the road from the Ghar Dalam Museum, there is a very large cave just off to the left of the road before reaching St. George's Bay. Two large blocks of apartments have been newly built on the top of the hill above a large, square opening framed in cement leading into the cave (576657). It can be found at the base of the slope on a line with the space between those two buildings.

The cave is about 25 feet wide and extends back and up for 150 feet or more. The bats, if they still roost there, are not present in the early evening as they would be out feeding. A lamp is necessary to find the way, especially as the stone blocks strewn about on the floor are slippery, but the interior of the cave is otherwise easily accessible and most impressive and interesting.

Sheep's Cave (Ghar in Naghag)

Continuing on through Birzebbuga, out to Hal Far and taking the road marked to Hasan's Cave (which is not included here), one comes to where the road turns to the west above the cliffs. To the left below is a ravine called Wied il-Mixta (544638), which can be easily approached by foot.

At the head of this short ravine, is a cave with an opening some 7 feet high and 6 feet wide that recedes in a northerly direction some 35 feet. Although a skeleton, which was probably Punic, was found there, the cave was not a tomb but had been a dwelling as indicated by the pottery found there. It was mostly of the Copper Age, including the Mgarr, Ggantija and Tarxien phases. There was also some Bronze Age pottery.

To the west of this cave is also a small one at about the same level on the side of the ravine, which has a very narrow opening through which light shines dimly from a small rectangular window on the west side of the rock promontory in which the cave is located.

Cave of the Wind

On the east side of Wied Mixta (545636), behind a large boulder is an opening about 8 feet high and 5 feet wide leading into a cave. There is an excellent path running down for about 150 feet to an opening in the cliff about 50 feet above the sea. There is some light all the way down during the day but a lamp might be helpful, especially to observe the surroundings. The walls on either side, which are of smooth stone, curve outward from the path and here and there form rounded ledges. They reach up some 40 feet to a vaulted roof closed in by huge boulders. This delightful cave, with its fine view of the sea, may have been occupied by ancient man but, due to the presence of a soil deposit covering the floor, no evidence is visable.

Cave Above the Sea

This cave, which is a short distance to the east of the Cave of the Wind, can be reached only by climbing down the side of the cliff, where it recedes into an opening of the cave (546636), for about 20 feet. Equipped with a proper belt around the waist and attached to a nylon rope secured to an iron pin driven into the rock surface above, the descent is not dangerous and is fairly easy for those sure of foot.

The cave is Y shaped, having two openings into the cliff about 200 feet above the sea. It extends back around to the right of some fallen rocks for about 50 feet or more. To explore its interior, a lamp is necessary.

As current excavations have shown by the abundance of sherds found there, Borg in-Nadur (Middle Bronze Age) people lived or worked there producing pottery. There are still some areas to be excavated that may bring to light Copper Age and Neolithic pottery and thus prove that the cave had been inhabited from the earliest times.

Ghar il Kbir Caves

Above Buskett, by the side of the large pattern of cart-ruts which are called Clapham Junction after the railway marshaling yard in London, there was until 140 years ago a very large cave surrounded by a number of large and small ones (455678). They housed a whole village, which was identified as such on the map of Malta. The very large cave, as painted by Brocktorff in 1827, was like a domed bazaar, filled with dozens of people meeting and exchanging goods.

15

These caves had certainly served as dwellings in the Bronze Age and possibly in the Copper Age and the Neolithic Period as well. The earliest recorded description of this village was in 1637 when a French visitor came to Malta. He wrote how at the entrance of the cavern he met a large number of men, women and children, dressed simply in the traditional garb of Maltese peasants. They were tall and broad, full of health and commonly lived to a ripe old age, and the women were well proportioned and beautiful in looks. They lived principally on vegetables, bread baked in their own ovens, cheese and fresh milk. They never consumed poultry, mutton or beef, but sold their livestock for slaughter in order to purchase their clothes, etc. These cave dwellers retained an original Maltese language similar to Lebanese, and could follow Mass which was said in Arabic.[9]

Around the large cave were a number of small caves, each the dwelling of an individual family; they were divided into a place for sleeping, another for storing provisions, and stalls were supplied for their cattle, sheep, donkeys and poultry. A place was provided for a hearth with an opening in the ceiling to let out the smoke, and there were also shafts for ventilation and to allow the daylight to penetrate the innermost recesses which were so made that neither the rain nor the wind could come in. And finally, to add colour to their walls, they were hung with garlands and clusters of onions and garlic.

In 1835, however, the British Government felt compelled to require these cave dwellers to leave their ancient homes and to reside in a modern village. This was achieved only with some difficulty and it happened that shortly after their removal, the very large cave and the next largest completely "fell in", so that it was not possible for its former residents to return.

Today, Ghar il Kbir is a labyrinth of caves surrounding what now reminds one, when viewed straight on from the top of its eastern perimeter, of the ruins of some ancient castle. Behind, on the far left, are the ruins of the second largest cave which is now used to shelter a herd of goats. In front to the left, and beyond the ruins of the largest cave, is a circle of rather large caves receding under the side of the hill, which apparently had been used to shelter donkeys and horses. Smaller caves continue around to the right side on the north. Half way along is a cave that was once used to mill grain; it is circular and around its edge is a well worn path where many a poor donkey must have trod out his life. In the centre, holes have been cut into the live rock, both into the floor and the roof, apparently to hold the mill from which a large shaft must have extended out to the edge of the cave.

Going on down to the right corner on the northeast, beside a path that borders the caves along the north side, a large hole has been cut into the live rock to form

[9] "Malta's Heritage", by E. R. Leopardi, 1969, pp. 30–32.

a channel down to a deep shaft that once had been the entrance to a Punic tomb, but which now serves as a cistern. Following the path to the west, it passes alongside a further series of caves, and in the deep and dark recesses of one may stand a patient, lone donkey looking out.

Dingli Cliff Cave

At the top of the hill above Ghar il Kbir, and down on the side of the cliff is a large cave (455672), which is divided to house two or three families and is provided with hearths and banks, niches, etc.

Xemxija Cave

In the side of the ridge, on the west side of its apex above some Mgarr/Ggan-tija tombs, is a cave dwelling (446789) which might have housed two or three Copper Age families. It has a wall extending across the centre, banks cut into the sides and hearths in three places in the floor.

Il-Latmija Cave

About 100 yards down from a wagon road along the north side of the western half of Marfa Ridge is a large karstic depression about 100 feet in diameter (395878). Entering it by a ramp on the north, one finds on reaching the level floor some 40 feet below that a canopy on the south side extends out for about 50 feet leaving a large, semi-circular cave. The interior of the upper part of the cave, which is formed by the remaining surface of the rock plateau, slopes down gradually at its rear to within a few feet of the floor. With such a natural protection from the elements and still affording plenty of light, ancient man had taken advantage of this ready abode and possibly a dozen families lived there at a time over hundreds if not thousands of years. They made a number of recesses and niches in the walls, some for small lamps and some like shelves for storing food, etc. There were places around the inner edge of the floor for hearths. One large recess, which has been cut into the wall, suggests it might have been the private chamber of the chief (figure 2).

Ghajn Abdul

Sherds of the Ghar Dalam phase have been found in a series of some twenty caves under the western rim of the butte above the spring called Ghajn Abdul in Gozo (287897).[10] Most of these caves were originally simply large openings in the side of the hill which were filled in with large stones, and adjoining them are often large recesses extending ten to twenty feet. One large cave has been partitioned by a stone wall extending to the ceiling some twenty feet above and

[10] Trump, 1972, p. 163.

a part is divided as well into three sections by low rubble walls, each apparently for a family and with a hearth for each. In the centre section is a bank some 15 feet across the rear wall, in front of which the floor is laid with flag stones. These caves were not an ideal dwelling but being so numerous, they could accommodate possibly 50 families.

Hilde Pirotim Lewis

2. Il-Latmija Cave

Santa Verna Caves

In the side of a cliff (338895), a few feet out from the remains of the Santa Verna temple in Gozo where Ghar Dalam sherds were also found,[11] there is a series of caves, several of which have been divided by low, rubble walls, or recessed in the floor, to provide dwellings for three families, each with a hearth.

HUTS

The only evidence of a village of huts prior to the Bronze Age that has come to light is that which was excavated by Dr. D. H. Trump at the site of the Skorba Temples (438754). The village had at various times included huts of both the Neolithic Period and the Copper Age. These excavations are located off the left side of the road in a field just a 100 yards beyond the limits of Zebbieh.

Of an Ghar Dalam hut discovered at Skorba, only the western wall has survived but it appears to have been oval and to have measured 15' in width and at least 20' in length. The wall is of stone but only $2\frac{1}{3}'$ thick, which would suggest the superstructure was of light materials, such as thatch, and from the discovery of an inverted quern in the centre of the floor it appears it may have contained a pole to support the roof. The floor was rough and probably had been covered with reeds or brush. In addition to this hut, an Ghar Dalam wall was discovered which is straight and measures 36' in length; there was also a hint of a cross wall extending out from under one of the Copper Age temples. It consisted of two layers of stone, mainly placed on edge and filled with rubble as is the custom in Malta even today; it measures 2' to $2\frac{1}{2}'$ in thickness.[12] From the debris inside the wall, it appeared that some lightly built huts had been enclosed by it whose superstructure was composed of wattle and clay. As what is still evident of the walls as well as the hut is rather confused, it would be possible to trace out what remains only by using the diagram in Dr. Trump's account of the excavations entitled "Skorba", published in 1966. The Ghar Dalam excavations are located within the area which is enclosed by a wire fence but the key may be obtained from the National Museum in Valletta.

In the way of building construction during the following phase 300 years later, called the Grey Skorba,[13] only the scanty remains of what may have been a wall were observed.

However, the remains of the Red Skorba Phase (4400–4000 B.C.) were more indicative of the construction of huts. The floors of these huts, which are outside the enclosed area, just to the right of the path and the wall in front of the gate,

[11] Trump, 1972, p. 158.
[12] Trump, 1966, p. 24.
[13] Trump, 1966, p. 30.

give a good idea of their size. Because of the contents found on them, it has been concluded that these huts must have had a religious significance and are therefore called the "Red Skorba Shrine". These huts consisted of four parts. The main room was oval and measured internally 28' × 18'. Adjoining it was a small D shaped hut measuring $18\frac{3}{4}'$ × $10\frac{2}{3}'$, which had no entrance. It will be noted that the floors of both have not been levelled. Next to these huts were two courtyards, which probably had no roofs but were stone paved. The walls

3. *Red Skorba Figurine*

of these huts averaged $2\frac{1}{8}'$ thick and apparently had been extended upward by using mud bricks. A great quantity of pottery was found in the two rooms, including fragments of stylized figurines (figure 3), and some twenty tarsals of cows of which the points had been ground off. In addition, they contained six goat skulls from which their face bones had been cut off. It is assumed that all of these objects had been votive offerings. They are on display at the National Museum.

The remains of clay floors of Zebbug Phase huts were found at a number of places in Skorba. The floor of one hut had been replaced twice, the lowest level being of mud-brick. Traces of a wall were also found cutting into a Red Skorba deposit and the corners of others were discovered. Clearly defined hearths were found in several Zebbug Phase huts.

Evidence of an Mgarr Phase hut, having a sub-rectangular plan and measuring $13\frac{1}{2}'$ across was also found at Skorba. It originally had a floor with a thin red streak of clay and ran to a substantial stone wall and there was apparently one across it. A part of the hut had been restored at a higher level, consisting partly of clay and partly of torba (a cement made of ground globigerina limestone).

Two Ggantija huts were found at Skorba representing what had been a considerable village both before and during the time of the temples. One was named the "Hut of the Querns" because eleven querns were found there; it was roughly rectangular and measured 20' × 10', built largely of mud-bricks and having a floor of beaten earth or clay. The other hut was named the "Hut of the Hollow" because of a large depression in the floor 10" deep. Its floor had been surfaced with clay and it was almost entirely intact; it measured 13' × 12'.

An excavation of six trenches by Dr. Trump in the field adjoining the back of the Borg in-Nadur (575655) defence wall on the south and near the end of its extension on the west, revealed a part of a hut wall. This was extended to expose the complete base of one hut and a part of another, both of which were oval.

20

They had floors of torba and a superstructure made possibly of wattle and thatch. One hut had flimsy walls measuring 25' × 11' 8". Inside it were hearth, a roller and a quern. The other hut, which was better built, was 11' 8" × 10'; it had had two different torba floors. A bench was found along one side which contained also a hearth, that was divided off from the rest of the hut by a dressed slab of stone with a recessed face (taken, no doubt, from the Copper Age temple there), which may have served as a base for a screen between the two parts of the hut. Excavation of the floor of the older hut, which had been abandoned when the other had been built, showed the following (in reverse) stratification: 1. A thin layer of soil containing Early Bronze Age (Tarxien Cemetery) sherds above the live rock; 2. Occupation debris with Tarxien Cemetery sherds mixed with early Middle Bronze Age (Borg in-Nadur) type sherds; and 3. Borg in-Nadur type sherds alone. On the floor of the newer hut was found pottery of late Borg in-Nadur ware including eight pots which had been smashed (apparently it was a superstitious custom to smash all pottery, which had been broken or when abandoned, during all prehistoric periods as well as the early historical).

GIRNAS

The girna, which is to be found spotting the valleys throughout the less cultivated areas of the island, is used today only as a shed for draft animals during the day and for storing hay. When it was first built on Malta is not known but those on Sardinia, which are more of a beehive shape and possibly 20' in diameter and as high, are apparently regarded as possibly prehistoric. Its architectural form is that of a corbel vault (figure 4). It is made by placing flat, but fairly

4. A Girna

21

rough stones around in circular rows, the lowest being about 10' in diameter, each of which is slightly narrower than the one below it, until it reaches a height of about 8'. It is then capped with one to four large, flat stones, depending on the remaining opening. The roof is covered usually with gravel and cemented with torba. No mortar is used in the construction of its circular wall and generally the only cross support is a stone lintel over the doorway.

A double girna below Ghajn Znuber (411788) in Malta, which has a wall running across a few feet in front of it, suggests an attractive, although unusual cottage, which it might well have been some hundreds of years ago. Whether its form inspired that of the megalithic temples of the Copper Age or vice versa or whether it even existed at that time can only be surmised but in view of the similarity of its architectural concept and its ingenious means of construction, the girna could well be, like the megalithic temples, a heritage of the unusually advanced people of that period.

CHAPTER III

MEGALITHIC TEMPLES

The development of the Age of the Temple Builders, which represented one of the most important cultural revolutions in antiquity,[1] was first identified in Malta from pottery found in graves at Ta' Trapna, a mile west of Zebbug, which proved to date from about 4000 B.C., and indicated a distinct cultural advance.[2] As shown by these graves, moreover, it had become the custom, unlike the Neolithics before them, to bury their dead collectively in tombs. The rock-cut chamber type of tomb, which was then introduced in Malta, was undoubtedly of eastern origin, being found in Cyprus, the Cyclades, Peloponnesus and Crete.[3] Aside from the fact that Malta remained dependent on flint and obsidian for tooling the soft and the relatively soft limestones for its surface structures and cutting their rock tombs, such as at Xemxija, it seems practically certain that this period, which is technically known as the Copper Age, was ushered in by a new race of people who soon assimilated the earlier Neolithic inhabitants.[4]

The Zebbug Phase, which is called after the village of Zebbug, near which their tombs were discovered, lasted until about 3600 B.C. In addition to their pottery which identified this new culture, one of the most striking finds was a stylized head carved from a piece of globigerina limestone (figure 5); also some axes of foreign

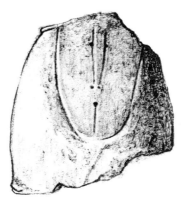

5. Zebbug Carved Head

---

[1] Brea, 1966, p. 58.

[2] Trump, 1972, p. 86.

[3] Brea, 1966, p. 63.

[4] J. D. Evans, "Malta in Antiquity", Blue Book—Malta 1968, p. 12.

23

polished stones were found in Zebbug deposits at Skorba, together with spindle whorls of terracotta which gave evidence of the continued improvement of spinning and implicitly of weaving as well.[5] The following phase called the Mgarr Phase, was transitional and lasted only about 100 years. Other than some refinements found in their pottery, statue-stelae, similar to those found in Troy I, were developed in Malta at that time, and the apotropaic symbol found at Troy, also came into use in Malta in the Mgarr Phase.[6]

The Ggantija Phase, which followed the Mgarr Phase in 3500 B.C. and lasted to 3000 B.C., was the first and greatest period of construction of the magnificent megalithic temples; it was never again equalled in experimental conception and it was outstanding for its cultural advance in general. Pottery was brought to a peak not equalled again in prehistoric times; it was noteworthy for its great variety of original designs. Spindle whorls of the Ggantija Phase were found at Skorba and also a convex bobbin with splayed ends, indicating an advance in the weaving industry which was already important.

Following the Ggantija Phase, there was a transitional one which lasted only about 100 years, and was called after the most beautiful of all temples, the Hypogeum, which was built at Hal Saflieni during that time. The development of pottery during the Saflieni Phase, in which the influence of the Ggantija Phase could still be detected, already gave evidence of the development to come in the Tarxien Phase; the exuberance of the Ggantija Phase had ended, while attempts to revive that great inventive period of the Copper Age seem to have been abandoned.[7]

The Tarxien Phase, which extended over a period of about 500 years from 2900 to 2400 B.C., is remarkable for its volume of output but not its qualitative development. The pottery tended to become stereotyped, and though there were attempts at innovation, they were no longer inspired.[8] Except for some temples constructed in the Early Tarxien Phase, it became apparent that they were no longer experimental but tended toward standardization, indicating a general decadence of the Copper Age culture which finally resulted in its disappearance.[9]

GENERAL DESCRIPTION

The construction of temples began with a comparatively small temple, such as that Kordin III E and Mgarr E, i.e., the so-called lobed temple composed of a

[5] Trump, 1966, pp. 14, 35–38.
[6] Brea, 1966, p. 62.
[7] Trump, 1966, pp. 14, 38.
[8] Trump, 1966, pp. 14, 38.
[9] Trump, 1966, pp. 43, 51.

central court surrounded by irregularly formed chambers, making a D shaped composite. Then followed the trefoil temple with three apses opening regularly into the court except later the central apse was often walled off. Subsequently, the five apse temples were developed, having a kidney shaped additional pair of apses at the front. Both types of temples were all constructed in the Ggantija Phase, except for one now placed in the Saflieni Phase. In addition, there were a number of four apse temples all of which but one were constructed in subsequent phases, a six apse temple of the Tarxien Phase, and various temples of anomalous forms belonging to the Ggantija and Tarxien Phases.[10]

Altogether, about ten temples were constructed during the Ggantija Phase, four, in addition to the Hypogeum, during the Saflieni or Early Tarxien Phase, and some two dozen in the Tarxien Phase. In Malta, the combined total exceeded two dozen and there were up to a dozen in Gozo.[10] Of these, most are grouped, i.e., there are four at Tarxien, three at Mnajdra, and there are ten places with two each, indicating, no doubt, the persistence of some communities, led by ambitious priests, to build more, as well as bigger and better temples, than their neighbours.

This spiritual and communal driving force for the extensive development of these magnificent megalithic temples, carried out in isolation by limited numbers of people and free of foreign influence, appears to account for this unique and outstanding achievement in antiquity.

With the possible exception of the Hypogeum, which was essentially a mausoleum and chapel, the temples were the religious centre of the community and they were not used for any other purpose although they could have served as strongholds in case of attack. They were apparently run by and directed by the priests who carried out many functions serving to propagate their religion[11] and incidentally to maintain their own leading positions in the community.

Among these functions, no doubt, the first was to encourage the construction and furnishing of the temples. The furnishings were quite elaborate. Besides the huge image of the Goddess of fertility and smaller images, they included beautifully decorated altars for sacrifice of animals and for secluded devotion, excellent reliefs on stone blocks, and decorated blocks and upright slabs throughout the temples, all of which were of local production apparently, bowls for burning incense, offering cups for libations, and even the knives used in sacrifices. Among the main functions of the priests, no doubt, was the performance of the sacrifice ritual[11] for which a fee was probably charged. Also, they served as oracles for the devoted, probably similar to that at a later date in Delphi, which being a noise made by a jet of gas, it is said, was interpreted by the priest in a vague way, subject to being understood in various ways. For this purpose, there

[10] Trump, 1972, p. 26.
[11] Trump, 1972, p. 30.

were chambers, either between the inner and outer walls or outside the temple, with holes in the inner wall through which the oracle's voice could be heard.

The main entrance as well as those to the various apses were supplied with curtains, probably of leather, to afford privacy, but until the construction of the six apse Central Temple at Tarxien, near the end of the Tarxien Phase, it appears the temples were usually open to the public as churches are today. Then a wall was constructed in several trefoil temples as well to close off the innermost apse.[12] The effect, no doubt, was to divide these temples into a private central apse at the end of the temple from the side apses which were left open to the public. This change could have been made, of course, to reserve the central apse as the altar is separated from the rest of the church today, where the devotion ritual could be carried out by the priests undisturbed. However, such a division of these temples to exclude the public from the central apse is thought by some observers to indicate an entrenched priesthood which, finding the public becoming restless, preferred to seclude themselves unmolested behind walls.[12] This assumption seems to be supported particularly by the separation of two whole kidney shaped pairs of apses in the Central Temple at Tarxien from the large pair just inside the entrance of that temple.

Several models of the exterior of the temples have been found. One is cut into an inner entrance screen at Mnajdra's Middle Temple, which shows only the facade, and some showing their complete outer form are on display at the National Museum. According to some of the latter, the temples were somewhat oval in shape with slightly rounded corners and roof. Another model, which has been restored from two pieces, suggests a fine neo-classical design.[13] However, it appears, from the ruins seen today, that most of them are like a horseshoe with a concave facade in the traditional form of the "Gate of Horn", while the smaller ones are in the shape of a D. The facade, on either side of a large trilithon entrance, was constructed of large upright slabs, over a horizontal bench extending forward, and bearing horizontal blocks. On the sides of the temples were very large, uneven and roughly cut slabs. To transport large slabs to the site of the temple, spherical stones about a foot in diameter, were used as rollers. Usually the stones used for the exterior were of harder coralline limestone while the interior stones were of the softer globigerina limestone. Between the outer and inner walls of the temples, was an area of about 2 to 15 feet wide, which was filled with rubble of all kinds, including sherds, etc, all without mortar as were the walls. The interior walls around the central corridor, apses and niches were lined with large, upright slabs supporting large, horizontal blocks; and the entrances to the apses were of large trilithons consisting of upright slabs with a large capstone between them

[12] Trump, 1966, p. 51.
[13] Trump, 1972, p. 28.

and flanked by large screens of stone extending out from the walls. As an exception to this rule, some of the oldest temples had the upper part of their inner walls of boulders rather than rectangular blocks. In all cases, the rows of the blocks or boulders, making up the upper part of the inner walls, were each placed so that they extended slightly into the interior, thus forming the base for a corbel vault. In some cases, the temples appear to have had an additional story or two but none has survived. There is no direct evidence of how the roof was constructed, for they have all fallen in and disappeared. However, they could not have been of large, flat stones, even if the walls could have supported them, as in the case of the farm sheds, formed without mortar into a corbel vault with flat stones on top, for none were found when the temples were excavated. In as much as the individual apses, niches and even the central corridor were all such that they could be closed in at the top by long beams, it is supposed, however, that this was done and that a single roof for the whole temple was placed over them, which was composed of brush and other light materials and cemented with ground globigerina, called torba, to make it waterproof. From the evidence remaining in some temples, the interior was plastered and painted with red ochre. The floors were either of the live rock or slabs generally, but in some cases they were paved with gravel and torba.

It is said that the form of the temples was copied from the rock-cut tombs at Xemxija, which preceded them[14] but perhaps it was that at Nahhalija, or the farm shed (Girna) having a corbel vault in its interior. However, Gertrude R. Levy has advanced a further theory as to their origin.[15] She attributes their stylistic ancestry to that of the cave and suggests that the model incised on the entrance screen of the Middle Temple at Mnajdra may be a variant of the plan of the interior passages often depicted at the threshold of Stone Age caves or tombs. The lack of a chosen orientation, moreover, she observes, strengthens the impression that the perpetually curved walls and the domed and vaulted roofs are reminders of the cave sanctuaries of a former ritual. Also, she points out, the orthostatic central corridor extending from the entrance through the whole length of the temple is straight like the usual passageway of dolmenic tombs, and that the setting of the pillar tables and altars with cave like recesses resembles tomb architecture. These, she states, are accounted for, in a place of public ceremony, where there is no corpse, by a cave nostalgia of Mediterranean burials. She goes on to say that the custom of placing a large temple alongside a small one may possibly embody the cult of a Mother Goddess and a young "Dying God" for a constant duality in which even the temples resemble a seated

---

[14] Trump, 1972, p. 27.
[15] G. R. Levy, "Gate of Horn", published by Faber and Faber Ltd., London, 1946, pp. 131–8.

figure; the head being at the axial dolmenic shrine and the shoulders and knees are formed by the pairs of lateral apses, while the large threshold stone resembles the base of the statue. In this way, she suggests it seems possible that, with the temples being erected as the bodies of the Gods, their form called up the divinity. Finally, she maintained that, with the temples being planned like a human body and the holy of holies situated at the head, only a people intellectually awakened could have conceived the divine power as concentrated there, as if their lives were concentrated in the king, and that the emblem of sovereignty should be regarded as a temple of the brain.

The most outstanding of what remains of the temples are those at Tarxien, the Hypogeum, Hagar Qim, Mnajdra, Ta' Hagrat and Tas Silg in Malta, and Ggantija in Gozo.

TARXIEN TEMPLES

At Tarxien, are four temples. From east to west, they are the Early Temple, the East Temple, the Central Temple and the South Temple. The Early Temple, which was built in the Ggantija Phase, stands at the extreme right at the end of the compound. The East Temple was built in the Early Tarxien Phase, about 50 feet to the west, and the Central Temple, which was built in the Tarxien Phase, was placed between the East Temple and the South Temple, which had been built in the Early Tarxien Phase, and which fronts on a large court at the end of a wide, walled lane leading from the inner exit of the office and museum which forms the main entrance from the outside.

South Temple

The great trilithon, which has been restored, once was the main entrance at the centre of a large facade. In front of it are two holes of about 5" in diameter and joined below in a big slab of rock; this is presumed to have been for tethering a large animal before taking it into the temple for sacrifice. On either side of the trilithon are the large horizontal blocks that formed the bench supporting the uprights of the facade but now missing. In front of these are some spherical stones originally used for bringing the large slabs and pillars to the site. At the tip of the facade on the right is a large recess cut into a slab of rock with the two sides and the back left to form its low walls. Five holes were cut clear through the slab for some purpose; it is likely that they were for libations, but it must be supposed, that some kind of containers were inserted in the holes to hold the liquid.

Entering through the trilithon into the large corridor of the temple, which leads straight through to its end, we come upon an apse on either side. Just inside on the right is a copy of the lower portion of what was once a statue of a

28

6. *Statue of Mother Goddess*

very large, obese Mother Goddess that had been there when the temple was in use (figure 6).

Straight ahead, on the right of the corridor, is a copy of the altar found there which bears a beautiful design of coils on both its front and side panels. There is a stone plug to a niche in the front panel behind which a long flint knife was found that was used presumably for beheading animals for sacrifice. The decoration on the block to the right suggests thin bent branches with twigs extending out from them. On the left in the corridor is a pitted bowl, possibly for burning incense.

The apse to the left, flanked with orthostats, has small blocks on its floor decorated with copies of a frieze of domestic animals.

The entrance to the next pair of apses has large orthostats on either side, each with double V perforations, presumably to hold leather curtains. Stepping up on the large stone bank of the apse to the left, we see at its end a step to a pedestal altar.

Returning to the main corridor, we see a fine, large sillstone, beautifully decorated, at its end. Behind it is a trilithon altar on a raised niche flanked by walls curving forward and a row of small blocks on each side of the floor.

Entering on the right into a small apse, which has been opened to afford access to the Central Temple on its left, we see opposite what was once a window slab opening into a small shrine with an altar to its right.

Central Temple

To the left, through the entrance, is one of the best views in the Tarxien temples; a lovely, decorated sillstone, bordered by huge orthostats, stands on a large horizontal block, beyond which we see between two further pairs of apses, each smaller than that before it, and to a trilithon at the end.

The entrance is bordered by two huge slabs, which are flanked on the other side by large upright slabs, each with a hole probably meant for a bar to prevent access by the public when desired. Ahead is a low remainder of a large bowl, possibly also used for incense.

Entering the apse on the left, past a large block on the floor containing a mortar inserted into a hole, we see inside to the right a large copy of a bowl, for which there was no apparent special use. On the left side of the apse is a trilithon backed by a door through a stone with large portals. At the back of the apse is also a trilithon with a tremendous capstone.

Coming back to the sillstone blocking the main corridor, and leaving for the moment the apse opposite, we can step over it, although as indicated by the slight wear on the original now in the National Museum, this liberty was not taken by the devotees in ancient times whom the priests apparently meant to keep out. There are, moreover, holes in the pillars flanking the portals which, no doubt, were intended to hold posts across the entrance to make sure the devotees did not get through.

There is a small bowl in the centre of the corridor ahead and on the left is a decorated slab at the entrance of the apse. Its inner wall is fitted closely with large uprights but the horizontal blocks that rested on them are missing. To the left in the apse is a small restored altar.

Back in the main corridor to the left is a large, stone bank leading to a trilithon entrance to the next pair of apses. A small apse on the left, entered through portals, is likewise lined with closely fitted uprights on which the horizontal blocks have been replaced to indicate that they extended slightly inward to form a corbel vault. On the left is again a small altar.

On the left, at the end of the main corridor, is an interesting stone placed in a niche; it resembles one at the Hagar Qim Temple which undoubtedly represented a fertility symbol.

Across the corridor is a very small apse or rather what is left of it; through it runs a ditch lined with a low wall said to have been built in Roman times as part of a cellar, without, obviously, their being aware of the megalithic temple.

Turning back to the next pair of apses and entering that on the left, we note

30

that it has been beautifully preserved with closely fitting slabs, extending to their original height, and on the right is again a small altar.

Retracing our steps still further, and going across the next apse on the left we find a narrow corridor. Following it around we see on the wall the remaining portion of a bull design above a square hole cut into the wall, and farther to the left is a frieze of a sow and above it a bull. At the end is another hole in the wall, the purpose of which is unknown.

Coming back into the apse and turning to the right, we step up on a stone in which V shaped holes were made for tethering an animal, and come to the outside. Around to the left is a narrow flight of a few steps between the two temples which apparently served as an entrance for the priests to their inner sanctum. A look from the top affords a good idea of the layout of the apses below.

East Temple

Entering through the wide opening into this temple and going through the large portals on the right which are flanked by large slabs on the inside of the apse there, we note the excellence of its inner wall of uprights standing at their original height.

Going on to the final pair of apses and through the portals, each perforated with V shaped holes for holding curtains, as well as a further set of holes on the inside edges, we proceed to the entrance to the apse on the right.

In this apse, the inner wall of uprights contains a hole through it on the right which leads to an oracle's cubicle between it and the outer wall. There is also a large opening in the wall to the left centre in back of which there appears also to have been a cubicle.

Early Temple

Going out around and through the court on the east we find rows of small blocks remaining from the temple there which had four apses around a large central apse. Passing on the right what may have been a small altar, there is ahead a large, flat stone with two libation holes in it, indicating that this ritual had existed at least since the time of the first temples. On the left are three surprisingly large holes covering an open area of about 10 × 20 feet and 5 or 6 feet deep which may have been used for storing the bones of the deceased as was the case in the Hypogeum.

HYPOGEUM

The Hypogeum at Hal Saflieni, Paola, is an underground mausoleum combined with a temple. It is the best preserved and the most beautiful of all the outstanding megalithic temples of the Copper Age. It was formed out of the live rock by people who still depended on flint and obsidian for cutting the stone. When excavated in 1905, it was estimated that the bones deposited there were those of 7,000 people. It was discovered in 1902 when a house was being built under which a cistern was being constructed. From the sherds found there, it is estimated that the Hypogeum was constructed about 3000 B.C.

Entering through the office in which there is a small museum, we come to a flight of 33 steps going down to the first level. There is a narrow corridor there between the stone walls. Looking straight ahead we see a window in the wall of the Chapel. We are overwhelmed at such magnificent beauty achieved with only implements of stone, and so well preserved that it is difficult to comprehend that what we see is 5,000 years old.

Passing by the modern cistern on the right and down the steps with railings bordering them, we come to the entrance of the Chapel or so-called "Main Room". Stepping over the low rim of its wall, which is a bit difficult, and down onto its floor, we are surrounded by a room of such superb architecture we try to think of anything that we have seen before that compares with it — Ancient Greece, the tombs of the Etruscans, or was it in a dream which the room itself suggests.

There are windows in the walls on all four sides, cut as if they had frames. To the left, recessed from off the floor are some small niches and beyond to the right are some a bit larger which G. R. Levy suggested were used by devotees for communicating with the divinity while sleeping, as represented by the small

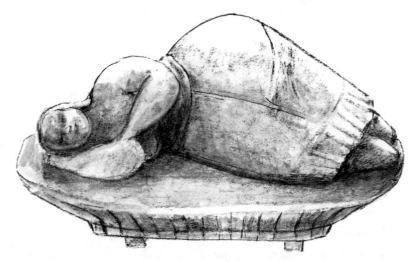

7. Statue of the "Sleeping Lady"

8. Hypogeum "Holy of Holies"

33

figure of the "sleeping lady" found there and now in the National Museum (figure 7).

Going to the end at the left and stepping down we come to a small cell and taking a step to the right we enter the rear room of the Chapel, called the "Holy of Holies", probably because it is so utterly beautiful in its architectural composition (figure 8). On its floor are two libation holes. Ahead is a recess which was probably for depositing bones. Then at the right end of this small chamber are some steps to the right going down to a lower level, while straight ahead are steps leading to the room beyond called the "Painted Room".

Taking the steps down to the right we come to a stone slab placed there since excavation, to allow for access over the deep pit below and going on to a corridor down some steps. There are several pits there on its side and at its end, all apparently for depositing bones.

Returning to the level above and going down steps to the right we enter a doorway with a large hole on its side which may have held a post across that entrance. Coming into the "Painted Room" we see on the wall on the left a number of coils painted in red ochre, at the right end of which is a group popularly described as "the tree of life". Turning and crossing to the right we see, looking through the wall and down, a deep pit called the "Snake Pit".

Entering into the next room or hallway, which is known as the "Unfinished Chamber", we proceed to the left and to the steps with railings leading down into the so-called "Oracle Room". The entrance, it will be noted, is through a window made in a slab of stone. Here there are designs painted in red ochre on both the left wall and the ceiling. To the left is a small pit, which may have been a depository for bones, while on the right is a large one and straight ahead is an entrance at the foot of the wall which is now cemented up. At the left end of the room up about four and a half feet is the niche known as the oracle. It is said that if a man speaks normally with his head reaching into it, his voice can be heard clearly at the corner of the room to the right of the steps, but that if a woman should try it, she would not be heard.

Returning to the so-called "Unfinished Chamber" and looking to the other end, there is a column standing free, made of the live stone. About the centre of this hallway is a corridor to the left. On its left is a trilithon entrance to a long pit at the end of which are piled splintered bones which were replaced there after excavation. On the right side of the corridor are two columns forming the entrance to an empty chamber. Farther on and up the steps is another chamber on the right, and straight ahead we come to an unfinished part of the Hypogeum. Straight ahead again there is a wall of new stones with a sign "No Entry". On the left is an opening into three low chambers. In the centre above one of them is what appears to be the biting end of an elephant's tooth, which would be almost 20 million years old; however, it is most likely the fossilized shell of a mollusc.

HAGAR QIM

The huge stones of the central temple of Hagar Qim stand gaunt and silent on a hill by the cliff on the west coast looking out to the tiny island of Filfla. There are actually four temples at the site but the two on the north and the one on the south-east are now little more than rows of megaliths. The central temple, on the other hand, is quite well preserved, except that the roof is missing, and it is to be noted that the horizontal blocks over the uprights in the facade were replaced after the temple was excavated in 1830. The temple may have been built in the Ggantija Phase (3500 B.C.) and was then composed of four apses; the fourth was later converted to permit a wide corridor and an entrance from the outside on the north. Four large oval apses were added on the west several hundred years later in the Tarxien Phase (2900 B.C.). This change in the original temple accounts for its non-traditional layout and what is now a strange maze of apses and niches divided by a central corridor running east-west and a narrower one extending from the main entrance. Having been extended, it is apparently the largest single temple of all, although the combinations of three temples at Tarxien and two at Ggantija are larger.

The facade at Hagar Qim is the most imposing of all the temples, although one or two others make a more powerful impression. The huge uprights are the originals as are the benches extending in front of them on both sides of the trilithon entrance. A few feet in front of the entrance are large holes joined below in the stone, which may have served to tether a large animal brought to the temple for sacrifice.

Entering through the huge trilithon, we come into a corridor between two apses. On either side of the trilithon, inside of the temple, are rectangular recesses with large blocks level with the floor; the one on the west contained the beautiful carved altar now in the National Museum and which has been taken as its symbol (figure 9). The floor of the corridor is covered with large blocks of stone while that of the apses on either side is composed of torba. The entrance to both apses is through a window cut in the stone and both are quite small and unimpressive, but the view of the wall outside the east apse is awesome.

Continuing on in the corridor, we come to a passageway with large

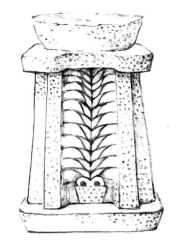

9. Hagar Qim Altar

35

portals, on either side of which are large blocks on the floor flanked by upright slabs. Entering through the passageway, we come to the east-west central corridor. At its right end is an apse containing a circle of thin slabs of stone, standing upright and imbedded in the floor. At the rear of the apse in one of the large uprights of the inner wall is an oracle's hole, behind which is a small cubicle. It is to be assumed that the devotees sat in the circle, leaning against the uprights carefully listening to the mumble of "wise" words coming through the hole. It is to be noted that there are very fine upright slabs in the inner wall of this apse, which are fitted closely, and that they bear the original horizontal blocks there which make a semicircle converging slightly toward the roof. Looking up toward the north side, we see standing high a kind of natural obelisk, 15 feet high, which is one of the most prominent features of Hagar Qim (figure 10).

The entrance from the outside on the north is bordered by large portals, flanked with huge upright slabs. The one on the left has two holes of about 5" in it and three of about 3" in which posts were probably placed when access by the public was not permitted. On the outside, the entrance is lined with smaller slabs, flanked by huge uprights.

Turning left in the main corridor and passing a large stone block on the floor to the right, we come to one of the most interesting combinations of installations to be found in any of the temples. On the right are two pedestalled altars and, as there are large blocks of stone beside them which could serve as seats, they look more like an outdoor restaurant. Going between them and entering over a step with V perforations for tethering an animal, and through portals, we come into a niche. Straight ahead is a kind of trilithon behind which is a small altar. To the left is another altar between portals. To the right is another niche in back of an entrance with portals which contains another two pedestalled altars, one of which has lost its table top. Beside it, to the left, in the larger niche is what was once an entrance between portals from the outside but now blocked.

Returning to the corridor, we see on the opposite side two large trilithons with huge capstones; there is also a large trilithon to the right.

At the end of the corridor on the left are some steps leading to an entrance bordered with portals and flanked by large slabs on the inside where there is an oval apse with a rough floor made originally of torba. Looking across the apse we see a window cut into a stone slab, behind which is a niche some 5 × 10 feet. To the right, we note the closely fitted uprights of the inner wall and, standing at the western end of the apse is a column which probably represents a phallus.

Returning to the corridor and turning to the left, we enter between two irregular slabs into an apse in which are a number of large boulders lying about on the floor; the uprights of the inner wall are quite high and there are horizontal stones across some of them. At the end of the apse, the uprights are broken and the exit to the outside has a portal on only one side. Just inside, on the floor, are

HildaBrohmLewis
Hagar Qim 1974

10. Hagar Qim

two stone blocks with deep holes in them, which apparently served as querns
for milling flour. Stumps of two Mother Goddess statues are outside on the right.

Coming back into the main corridor and again turning to the left, we step over
a sillstone with a single portal on the right, and enter an apse which is narrow
but fairly long. There are rather high uprights with a bench beneath those on the
right. To the left is a jumble of large stone blocks on the floor. On both sides of
the apse, it will be noted that for every two or more uprights placed facing the
apse, there is one placed sideways between them.

Stepping up at the end of the apse between low portals, we come to the outside of the temple. To the right and extending out from under the rear wall is a large bench of horizontal stones. Beyond are some steps leading to a small rectangular area, which, however, is blocked by a large slab at its rear.

Next is the outside and only entrance to a double apse contained in the north-west corner of the temple. Having once had an entrance from the inside and another from the outside, but now blocked, it seems the priests responsible must have been plagued by some uncertainty before setting up a sanctum to which the public was apparently not generally admitted. In front of its present entrance is a large slab, level with the ground, containing two libation holes, each about 8'' in diameter. On its right is a step and then a sillstone, followed by a stone floor in which again there is a hole for libations, all between portals containing perforations for curtains and flanked by low slabs. This double apse in which the uprights are well worn, has a floor of small blocks about a foot square. Looking across, we see what had been the entrance from the next apse, but now blocked. On either side are rectangular niches, flanked by pitted stone uprights and a large block on the floor.

Returning to the outside and turning to the east, we come to a small trilithon altar hidden on the right underneath. To the east of that is what had been an entrance but now blocked, that led into the niche behind the pedestalled altars. Its portals are flanked by pitted slabs and there is a large block on the floor in front with two libation holes of about 8'' each.

Passing the entrance of the temple on the north, we come to the mighty uprights of the outside wall, one of which is the high "obelisk" previously referred to. Below them, a row of horizontal stones forms a bench and that at the base of the "obelisk" juts out beyond the rest because this large upright had been placed sideways between the others. On beyond, recessed in the wall, is the cubicle where the oracle was apparently housed.

We now come to an outside shrine which is particularly interesting because of the fertility symbols of stone. The shrine is recessed into the outer wall of the temple behind portals on the outside with a stone floor between, and a second pair of portals is inside. At the back is a column, somewhat square in shape, which appears to have been a phallus. In front of it about two feet is another stone between a low bank on either side, which resembles a keystone but apparently was meant to represent a female figure.

Going on between a large boulder on the ground, in which there are libation holes, and the stone bench in front of the uprights of the outside wall, we note that the latter are particularly large; in fact, the slab at the southeast corner must be the largest of any in the temples; it is 23 feet long, some 14 feet high and about 2 feet thick, and weighs about 20 tons. Continuing around the corner we come back to the trilithon entrance where we started.

MNAJDRA TEMPLES

There are three temples at Mnajdra. The oldest, which is on the right, is called the Small Temple, dating from the Ggantija Phase. The Lower Temple to the far left is of the Early Tarxien Phase. And raised above, in the centre, is the Middle Temple which is of the Tarxien Phase. There is little left of the Small Temple but there is enough of the Lower Temple still to be seen to pronounce it architecturally the most impressive of all. The Middle Temple, which evidences the cultural decadence referred to previously, is much more simple in its concept and structure.

Small Temple

Entering the courtyard in front of the Mnajdra temples and looking up to the east, we see the Small Temple which originally had three entrances, all of which were within low portals, but now blocked with stone. We note that there were three apses which are now bordered with a modern wall of small stones. The small apse ahead, behind three upright stones flanked with low portals, is partly paved with torba.

Middle Temple

Crossing over the terrace in front of the Middle Temple, we come to its entrance, which originally was a window through a very large slab, now broken. There is also an entrance to its left and formerly there was one on the right which is now blocked.

Stepping up and through the broken window slab with low portals, we note a hole of about 4″ in one which could have held a pole to prevent access when necessary. There are low orthostats on either side of the portals.

Turning to the right, we enter a medium size apse. The closely fitted uprights, which are not too high, carry horizontal blocks of one or two layers. Returning to the corridor and crossing into the left apse, we find again closely fitted uprights lined with layers of horizontal blocks.

Coming back into the corridor we see the large slabs on either side of the entrance into the rear pair of apses and the recesses on either side in which there are stone blocks a foot high which were used apparently for preparing animals for sacrifice. To the sides of these are large slabs extending forward. On the side of the slab on the left is a model of the temple incised apparently when the temple was in use. It is about a foot wide and 9 inches high; its lower half is divided into three parts while the upper is divided into four layers making up the facade of the roof.

Entering between the portals, where there is a slab for the floor, we see large orthostats on either side and flanking them are slabs protruding into the next pair of apses. Stepping down on the floor which is of gravel and torba, we turn into a medium size apse on the right.

The inner wall of this apse is lined with closely fitted but low uprights holding a double row of horizontal blocks in a semi-circle with each row slightly protruding into the interior which would indicate that the apse originally formed a corbel vault.

Crossing over to the apse on the west, where there are closely fitted, low uprights covered with one or two rows of horizontal blocks, we note in the left centre of this apse a window in the stone lined with portals and standing on a large block of stone; stepping through the window, we come to a small chamber with a large pillar altar bordered with orthostats.

Returning to the apse, we see in the niche on the north a very large trilithon held up by large slabs and columns of new stones and flanked by large slabs extending forward on either side. In back of the trilithon are some large slabs of the outside wall and in a slab to the right are two toe holes which indicate there was once another story.

Lower Temple

Returning to the outside and retracing our steps in front of the terrace and beyond the Small Temple where there are steps, we cross the courtyard to the Lower Temple. Standing in front of the facade, which is one of the most magnificent on the islands, we note a trilithon to the rear of a pair of portals without a capstone forming the main entrance. It has wide steps in front and there is a wide stone bench extending on either side. In an upright on the right is a hole leading into the oracle's niche, indicating perhaps there was curb service for those in a hurry! To the left, the facade extends beyond the temple for about 20 feet. At its end is a large, flat block, which is rounded on its nearer edge but straight on its other three sides and was probably used for cermonial purposes; to its left is what appears to be the upper half of a large spherical boulder.

Entering the entrance up its steps, we note on the left a small conical stone embedded in another which probably represented a phallus. Continuing through the portals we see large orthostats on either side with blocks in front of each; the one on the east is pitted on its side. Turning to the left apse, we see a trilithon on the left with a raised floor. Farther on are large, closely fitted uprights on which there are two rows of horizontal blocks and a third has been fitted onto two of them. Below is a large block with smaller ones on either side, one of which is pitted.

To the right in that apse we come upon a very fine trilithon within which is a window in the stone, all being pitted. There are also large pitted slabs standing sideways on either side. Stepping through the window onto a block, we see ahead a large double pillar altar, about 8 feet across and each pillar is about 4 feet high. To the left is a smaller double pillar altar but with one pillar missing and one is to the right which is missing its upper pillar.

Returning through the window we cross over to the east apse which is closely fitted with uprights above which are three or four rows of horizontal blocks extending slightly inward. On the right, we come to the entrance of a shrine which is between the inner and outer walls, and go up three steps. There are two holes in the portals to hold a curtain and at their edge is another pair of such perforations. To the right is a trilithon within which is a window of stone (figure 11), and behind it is a kind of cabinet of stone. To the right is a square hole in the wall for the oracle and beyond is a broken altar.

Returning to the apse, we note a large block in the centre of the floor with a hole for libations. On the northeast in an upright is a hole extending into the oracle's niche between the inner and outer walls.

11. Mnajdra Trilithon Altar

41

In the centre, between the apses, is a large entrance in a trilithon to the next pair of apses, flanked by large slabs extending forward. On the near end of the slab on the left is a very interesting graffito made possibly by some early Christian in about the 4th century, when the front part of the temple was only partially covered with silt. It is a symbol of a fish within a geometric design of a square with a cross.

On either side, in front of the slabs are large, pitted blocks, each within a recess, flanked on the outside as well by pitted slabs.

Entering through the trilithon and stepping up on a block with a libation hole in it, we see on the opposite side of the apses a very large altar against the inner wall and between very large slabs. Stepping up on a large slab on the floor to the right into a small apse, we see its uprights are of irregular stones on which there are some rows of stone. Crossing over to the small apse on the west, we again see the pillar altar through an opening in the wall forming one of the group in the niche entered from the front apse.

Returning to the front entrance of the temple and going around to the back where the two temples join, we see where the oracle had his niche behind a large trilithon with a tremendous capstone weighing possibly five tons. Climbing up between the temples and looking to the left onto a top horizontal block of the inner wall of the Middle Temple, which is protected by an overhanging stone, we see cut into the stone what appears to be a very fine, tiny model of the Punic sanctuary at Ras il Wardija in Gozo. As the hard coralline stone does not deteriorate, especially when protected from the elements, we ask ourselves whether this beautifully cut little model could have been made by a Carthaginian in the third century B.C. when the sanctuary was constructed.

TA' HAGRAT

There are two adjoining temples at Ta' Hagrat in Mgarr. They are located on the edge of a cultivated field at the end of a short street running off the Mgarr–Zebbieh road two blocks east of the Police Station where the key may be obtained. A large iron gate is at the corner and a wide path leads down to the main entrance of the larger temple on the south. The big temple is trefoil and the smaller one on the right is lobed. The larger one on the left was constructed in the Ggantija Phase and the smaller one was added in the Saflieni Phase.

In front of the entrance to the larger temple is a spherical stone which was probably used to enable the huge megaliths to be brought to the site. Three broad steps are across the entire width of the imposing entrance. There are two huge trilithons each with a tremendous capstone. Both of the latter had to be put back in place after excavation; the one over the second pair of portals had been pushed forward at an angle and the other was found in the field in front.

The corridor between the trilithons is slightly recessed and is separated from the central corridor by a row of low stones. A border of stones about 10″ high frames the other sides of the central corridor.

The apse at the left has two large portals at its entrance, one of which is about 13 feet high. Its inner walls, made of uneven, boulder like stones indicate its early age.

The apse at the end of the corridor is without its portals and its inner wall is also made of irregularly shaped stones but the outer wall behind it consists of large, high slabs, cut into rectangular shapes.

The entrance to the apse on the right is flanked by low portals. Its inner wall on the south indicates it had been constructed to form the base of a corbel vault, but that on the north was removed to allow access to a flight of steps leading up between the inner and outer walls of the apse on the north to a former exit there. These steps were installed following excavation as it was considered that such steps had been there originally.[16] To the south, outside the inner wall of this apse and that of the smaller temple to the east, two pits, about five feet deep, were found but their purpose could not be identified.

On the east side of the east apse of the larger temple, the wall has been removed to allow access to the smaller temple. Its entrance is flanked by low remainders of its original portals. A corridor leads straight through to the rear apse to the east. The largest apse of this small temple is on the left; some of its inner wall is missing both in front and at its rear. Immediately to the right of the entrance of the temple is a small apse behind the remains of its portals and only a few megaliths of its inner wall are still standing. Beyond is a niche with portals but its inner wall is missing. Likewise, the entire outer wall of the small temple has long since been removed by farmers intent on widening the field for cultivation.

The outer wall of the larger temple, on the other hand, is standing for the most part, except for the original extension of the facade on the east where the path from the gate now passes. The facade on the west side has been extended out beyond the temple for some 30 feet. It consists of two rows of huge megaliths filled between with rubble, and it can be seen that the huge trilithons of the larger temple were once flanked by a mighty "Gate of Horn".

TAS-SILG TEMPLE

The temple at Tas-Silg, the excavation of which was basically completed in 1970 by the Missione Archeologica a Malta of the University of Rome,[17] is the

---

[16] Bulletin of the National Museum of Malta, February 1929, pp. 4–14.
[17] "Missione Archeologica A Malta", University of Rome, vols. 1963, 1964, 1965, 1966, 1967, 1969 and 1970.

only one of the three dozen or more Copper Age temples that is known to have continued in use as a complete structure after the catastrophic end of that age about 2400 B.C. That this temple survived may have been due to the fact that it was fairly new but also its oval shape may have made it more sturdy. Due to the survival of the temple, it appears that a small community of Copper Age people remained there, while all the rest apparently disappeared completely.

The temple area, which included a Phoenician-Punic-Roman sanctuary and a Christian convent centuries later (see Tas-Silg Sanctuary and the chapter on the Early Christians), is surrounded by a high wall built by the excavators but the key may be obtained at the Church to the southeast.

The foundations of the temple, which was built in the Tarxien Phase, are more or less complete except on the south side. The interior of the temple was of a four apse lobed construction and the outside wall with a bench projecting all around was basically oval with a concave recess for a facade back and front. The entrance on the southeast had a threshold with three libation holes. The main entrance was on the northwest, indicated by the fact that a carved figure of the Mother Goddess of fertility was found near it in the northwest apse. Also, there was a large door in the facade, which could probably be closed with curtains, that was flanked by large, rectangular stones imbedded in the live rock. There were, moreover, two lateral stones on either side, and before the entrance, there were two stout pillars beside a threshold of greenish-grey stone extending forward. This large stone appears to have been regarded as a particularly holy place.

The crescent shaped facade of the temple was extended out to the northwest where there is a large, rectangular stone basin, 15 feet in length and slightly recessed in the centre, apparently to be used in the rites of ablution. Beside it, still standing when the area was excavated, was a short column, representing a baetylus or holy stone, modelled to form a divine type of female, probably a priestess.

Forming the other side of a large semicircle running out from the facade of the temple to the southwest, was a trench now seen extending into the area within a wall on the other side of the road to Delimara, beside which at the end was another baetylus which was also still standing. With the baetylus on the northwest, it formed an optuse triangle, the sides of which were each about 100 feet.

In addition to this triangle extending out from the entrance of the temple, there were other structures on both the northwest and the southwest, which served partially or wholly to enclose the temple, making it a fulcrum for a number of courtyards joined to one another.

GGANTIJA TEMPLES

At the top of the new road to Xaghra is a wall lined, unpaved road leading back at a diagonal to the south around the entrance of the Ggantija Temples. They were excavated first in 1827, and thereafter sporadically until 1848. Then, they remained uncared for over a century, during which time they deteriorated generally and the interior fittings, which had been quite well preserved, were greatly damaged or disappeared entirely. There are two adjoining temples without communication between them. The larger and older one, dating from about 3500 B.C., on the southwest has 5 apses consisting of two pairs each joined in a kidney shape, and one at the end of the corridor. The smaller one, also built in the Ggantija Phase, on the northeast, has 4 apses, likewise consisting of two pairs each joined by a corridor, and a niche at the end.

The outer wall of hard coralline limestone, which encircles the rear and sides of both temples, is based on the technique of alternately placed slabs, one with its flat surface broadside and the other with an edge extending forward. These slabs, whose sides are most irregular, with the spaces between filled by smaller, flat slabs, form the uprights; they are placed on horizontal slabs which extend forward, and above the uprights are rows of horizontal slabs still standing on a good part of the wall, particularly to the left of the facade of the southwest temple. The facade to the left of the northeast temple has fallen down completely. There is a large entrance to each of the temples recessed in a concave semicircle.

The facade on the left of the southwest temple extends outward for some feet and is made of large upright slabs, but while the right side of the facade of the northeast temple also extends out, there are only small and medium megaliths remaining. Their outer arms thus embrace a large terrace in front of the the temples which no doubt formed a centre for outdoor rituals, high above the valley below.

The inner walls of the apses, which extend upward quite high, are composed almost exclusively of large, irregular boulders from the floor up. They appear to be rather primitive from the architectural point of view, especially as compared with the finely tooled upright and horizontal slabs in later temples. Originally, however, the space between them was filled in with plaster, painted red, and these apses were probably much finer than can be supposed from their present appearance.

The space between the inner and outer walls, varying from a foot to over 15 feet, was filled with rubble of all kinds, including bits of the oldest pottery of the Copper Age.

The entrances of the corridor, both at the front of the temples, and those leading to the rear pair of apses, are flanked by large slabs of globigerina limestone, which extend out, thus forming a wide frame for the entrances to all the apses in both temples.

Northeast Temple

To the left of the entrance to this temple, the bench, extending out from below the fallen down wall, has a V shaped perforation in its corner, apparently

45

intended for tethering a large animal before sacrifice. There is a large step across in front, followed by two blocks forming the floor of the entrance between portals. Each portal contains two holes, used probably for holding crossbars to prevent access when desired. The slabs flanking them likewise have a large hole apparently for the same purpose.

The apse to the right has, on the left side of its entrance, a niche between upright slabs, while on its right side is only a recess with a slab against the wall. The apse to the left also has a niche at its entrance on the right recessed between slabs, the right one of which forms a portal of the entrance to the next pair of apses.

Of the rear pair of apses, that on the right is elevated on two rows of stone blocks. At the end of the corridor is a niche on both sides of which are what apparently had been trilithon altars in front with a narrow passageway between. The niche raised about two feet forms a semicircular platform and its inner wall is backed against the outer wall, which is of huge, irregular slabs.

The apse on the left contains a large slab on the floor which is broken in a number of places, and apparently served for slaughtering animals for sacrifice on what had been a triple altar at the back of the apse; there remain of it only two low orthostats with blocks lying on the floor on either side.

Southwest Temple

The tremendous facade to this majestic temple reaches 20 feet on the left side; it is built up on irregular upright slabs on a bench of horizontal slabs. Across the top are five rows of horizontal slabs, most of which had been cut into rectangular blocks. In front of the left side of the facade are a number of spherical stones on which the large slabs were apparently brought to the site. Across the front of the entrance is a most remarkable slab, measuring 15 × 8 feet, which forms a step. Behind is a very low sillstone and on either side are the stumps of rather narrow portals standing in front of two large slabs. Just inside the entrance is a large block with a small basin cut into it. Across the inside of the entrance is another large block containing a hole for libations. At the edge of the slab uprights on either side are four holes in each to hold cross-bars. Behind, on the right, is a huge upright slab some 14 feet high.

In front of the apse on the right is a ring of small cobble stones forming the remainder of what had been a hearth probably for burning incense. Beyond is a semicircular step bordered on either side by rectangular blocks. That on the left still has the remainder of its decoration of coils but that on the right has been worn smooth by the weather. There is a further step leading up to what appears to be the remains of a trilithon altar placed on still a further step. The other blocks and fittings, several with decorations, as seen in Brocktorff's painting of 1827, have all disappeared.

The apse on the opposite side contains only two blocks on its floor made of torba, and a bowl at its rear.

The entrance to the inner pair of apses has a large step across, the near side of which bears a pitted design. There are double portals, the capstones of which are missing. The floor, which is paved with stone blocks, contains two libation holes. The end on either side of the entrance is flanked by large blocks beside which are large slabs extending outward.

The apse to the right has a low circle of stones on the floor, which probably formed a hearth for burning incense. Extending from the rear on both sides is a row of small stones probably once joined in a semicircle. To the left are some large blocks on the floor.

In the apse on the left are several large uprights by its left wall, followed by a row of closely fitted lower slabs and on the right side is a row of very low blocks. Across the back is a well preserved triple altar with four high uprights with horizontal slabs part way up between them, supported by three pillars in the centre and two original ones on either side.

At the end of the corridor is a small apse raised about two feet. It has a stone floor, the outer edge of which has a pitted design. The inner wall has some very large, irregular slabs at the base, over which are the usual irregular boulders. On the floor of this apse, some lines have been incised, which have been interpreted as an invocation in Phoenician. It is not likely that they are prehistoric, however, as the temple was probably covered by silt. Rather they are said by local authorities to have been made by a rather extraordinary man who in 1857 built the Church at Mosta and in 1826 attracted scientists and archaeologists from around the world by claiming that Malta could be the Lost Atlantis.

LOST ATLANTIS?

The Copper Age temples of Malta, which were unique in the Mediterranean and the world for that matter, and represented there a golden era of 1,600 years, are evidence of a people with a high degree of culture and engineering skills which was outstanding in their time. In fact, it might be supposed that Malta might have been Plato's Lost Atlantis described as a Utopia with a high civilization, on a large island in the western sea. Malta is not known to have been inundated by the sea since the ice age, it is not in the Atlantic beyond the Gates of Hercules, nor did it rule Lybia and Egypt, but it could have been all that was said of the Lost Atlantis from the viewpoint of its achievements.

L. Bernabo Brea, an outstanding authority on the antiquities of the Mediterranean, stated: "Malta, especially with its splendid Tarxien civilization and its extraordinary megalithic architecture, reached one of the peaks of culture and artistic progress in prehistoric Europe".[18]

Including the Neolithic Age, it appears that up to the end of the Copper Age, Malta had enjoyed an unparalled period of peace of more than two and a half

[18] Brea, 1966, p. 66.

millennia. There had been a considerable development of industry and trade, particularly in textiles which were exported to many countries, presumably as far away as Crete. As has been noted, there was a cultural decadence after the Saflieni and Early Tarxien Phases, when there were some excellent examples of megalithic structures, if not following already at the end of the Ggantija Phase. Also, there may have developed a restlessness among the population toward the end of the Tarxien Phase as indicated by the complete separation by a barrier at the Central Temple[19] at Tarxien of the first pair of apses from the remaining double apses of that temple. The extensive building of temples in the Tarxien Phase, moreover, may have sapped the strength of the population and undoubtedly lead to a denuding of the forests with a consequent erosion of the soil, less rain, intensified heat in the summer and a possible drought. Like the Knights of Malta in 1798, the Copper Age people may have outlived their time on Malta and needed only a catastrophy to drive them off the islands completely. Such a catastrophy could well have been an earthquake, which, according to Plato, destroyed the Lost Atlantis. That Malta was destroyed at the end of the Tarxien Phase in 2400 B.C. is evidenced by several factors. First, the break was sudden and complete, as there is no sign of the continued existence of people on Malta, except for a very small community at Tas-Silg. Secondly, there is evidence in the central court of the Central Temple at Tarxien of a widespread reddening of the stone which was undoubtedly the result of an intense heat as would be caused by the burning of a fallen roof with wooden beams, brush, etc., and of a similar conflagration at the West Temple at Skorba.[20] Thirdly, the destruction of all the temples, except the Hypogeum and a part of that at Tas-Silg, was so complete that they could not be occupied again except by squatters in the next period who made no attempt to restore them but used only their walls as protection from the wind. That the destruction led to the complete evacuation of both Malta and Gozo, except at Tas-Silg, is evidenced by a layer of silt, 2–3 feet deep, that had accumulated on the floor of the remains of the temples at Tarxien below a layer of sand which the Early Bronze Age (Tarxien Cemetery) people had deposited there for the cremation of their dead.

It is difficult to determine how long it had taken for the silt to accumulate before the Early Bronze Age (Tarxien Cemetery) people arrived on Malta. An outstanding authority stated there was something in the nature of an interlude before the next period began but observed only that it was not possible to determine the length of time.[20] However, it has been estimated that it might have been from 50–150 years.[21] Accordingly, 100 years have been taken arbitrarily as the hiatus between the two ages, although it could have been more.

[19] Trump, 1966, pp. 50, 51.
[20] Trump, 1966, p. 7 and 1972, p. 20.
[21] F. X. Mallia, Director of Museums, Malta.

CHAPTER IV

DEFENCE WALLS, DOLMENS, SILOS AND CART-RUTS

It is mainly from their defence walls, dolmens, silos and cart-ruts that the little that is known about the life of the Bronze Age peoples on Malta and Gozo has been gained. All three, the Early Bronze Age (Tarxien Cemetery), the Middle (Borg in-Nadur), and the Late (Bahrija), who came to Malta and Gozo during this age, must have been refugees who apparently had been driven to these islands by fear of other tribes and lived here in fear of foreign marauders over hundreds of years. The islands were desolate and barren when the few Early Bronze Age people arrived but there was apparently no marked improvement by the time the Middle Bronze Age people joined them or even when the Late Bronze Age settlers came. They probably could have at best eked out only a bare living in any event but preferring the frugality of safety, they all sought out the isolated and less accessible ridges and promontories where, behind defence walls of large stones, they placed their settlements, even though the rocky terrain offered little prospect of fruitful cultivation or grazing for more than a limited number of animals. The silos of the Middle and Late Bronze Age people bespeak of the necessity of conservation of food and, with their increasing numbers, they became important, along with the bell shaped tombs remaining from the Copper Age, as reservoirs for storing water in the dry season. And the cart-ruts indicate that, notwithstanding the privations, they continued to live on the barren ridges and promontories until even long after the Phoenician-Punic Age brought them greater security and an advanced culture. Finally, the dolmens, as well as their urn fields, give evidence of an apparent lack of man power and energy in that they could only resort to cremating their dead instead of inhumation in rock-cut tombs as had the Copper Age people before them and probably their forebears from whence they had stemmed.

The Early Bronze Age on Malta, which may have begun about 2300 B.C., appears to have been brought about by a completely new race of people. Like the people of the Copper Age, they had come from the Peloponnesus, where a few remaining huts of a Middle Helladic (2250–1900 B.C.) village at the present site of Olympia were found containing pottery similar to that made by the Tarxien Cemetery people,[1] but they had not originated in Anatolia as their predecessors had. They were apparently a Caucasoid subracial group that had stemmed chiefly from Eastern Europe, especially Yugoslavia and Albania, and being round headed, while the Copper Age people were long headed, it is considered that they were probably Dinaric.[2]

These people came westward from Mainland Greece about the same time to Castelluccio in Sicily and Lipari (Capo Graziano) in the Aeolian Islands, as well as to Malta; all were of the same origin as indicated by the similarity of their pottery to that of each other as well as to that of the village of Olympia. In addition, some of these people may have come to Otranto in southern Italy as well as is indicated by dolmens there similar to those in Malta.

The Early Bronze Age (Tarxien Cemetery) people, as stated at the end of the previous chapter, had cremated their dead at the Tarxien Temples. When excavated, a deposit of sand on the floor of the ruins consisted of dark soil, ashes, etc., including burial urns, which had become broken, but had contained the cremated remains of bodies and various objects still to be found in the deposit. The bodies were dressed or wrapped in fine or coarse cloths, dyed a deep yellow, and the various objects included different types of pottery, ornaments, especially faience beads, and, most interesting, copper axes and flat daggers covered with carbonized grasses and seeds. Thus, these deposits not only gave evidence that these people had cremated their dead but also that they had belonged to the age of metal, i.e., the "Bronze" Age.[3]

That the Tarxien Cemetery people cremated their dead while the corresponding culture at Castelluccio in Sicily had buried their's is, according to archaeologists,[4] not considered important, as it appears quite normal for one branch of a corresponding culture to cremate their dead while the other buried them.

It is significant, however, that although the Tarxien Cemetery people had limited quantities of metal, they appear to have represented a less developed culture, particularly as evidenced by their pottery. One is grey ware, sometimes decorated with dot-filled zigzags and is coarse in texture; it was identified upon excavation as "archaic": Many of the pots found at the Tarxien Cemetery were reported to have been "rough, thick and greyish in colour, being black in fracture which showed poor baking".[3]

Most interesting among the artifacts found at the Tarxien Temples are a group of discoid figurines (figure 12). They are of brown ware with a burnished surface,

[1] Brea, 1966, p. 100.
[2] Trump, 1966, p. 49.
[3] Evans, 1971, pp. 150, 161.
[4] Trump, 23.2.1975. Personal letter.

50

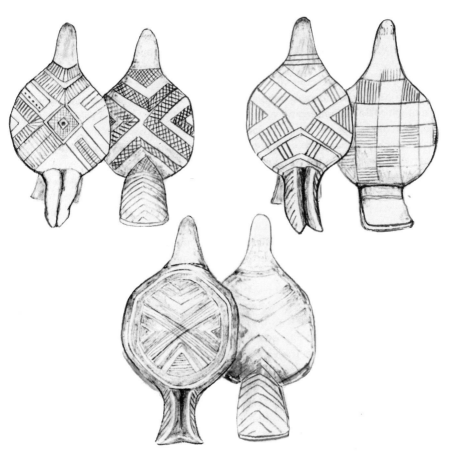

12. Early Bronze Age Figurines

an elaborately incised decoration and with tiny, stubby legs. The decoration is composed mainly of V shaped and horizontal bands filled with cross-hatching. Also interesting are three small models of "birds", also done in dark, brown clay with a polished surface, a decoration of deep grooves and cross-hatching all over.[3] All are on display at the National Museum.

The origin of the Middle Bronze Age people, who are called Borg in-Nadur after that of the ridge running up from Birzebbuga, on which their pottery, etc., were first found, has not been definitely identified. However, D. H. Trump states: "Borg in-Nadur appears not to have developed in Malta, Sicily is nearest and has hints, nowhere else has yielded anything better".[5]

[5] Trump, 23.2.75.

One of the best hints is the Capo Graziano culture of Lipari in the Aeolian Islands. It had a long life which lasted until the beginning of the next period, i.e., about 1500 (1400?) B.C. There was no equivalent phase in Sicily, and Lipari evidently had few contacts with the main island at that time as the Castelluccio culture was no longer contemporary with it.[6] On the other hand, it had close links with the Tarxien Cemetery people in Malta.[7] Tarxien Cemetery pottery was like that of the Capo Craziano culture and was found in large quantities on the island of Ognina in the Bay of Syracuse where they must have had a trading post already during that period.[8] It appears there must have been a significant trade between the two, exchanging obsidian for pottery.

Excavations on the Lipari acropolis showed the Middle Bronze Age village there had been destroyed by fire,[9] and colonized by the Ausonians from the Italian Mainland thereafter. Having been deprived of their homes, and being in close contact with the Tarxien Cemetery people, it would seem quite possible, therefore, that the people of Capo Graziano should have taken refuge in Malta where there were but few people and they would have been relatively safe.

The newcomers seem to have amalgamated with the Tarxien Cemetery people already on Borg in-Nadur, as shown by their respective pottery there,[10] and in due course, produced a distinctly different type of pottery which they exported to Sicily, using again the island of Ognina as their outlet. Some of their wares were sold to the villages of the Thapsos culture north of Syracuse in whose tombs they have been found.[11] The Thapsos culture, which is thought to have developed from earlier related cultures in northeast Sicily, which also gave rise to the Milazzese culture in the Aeolian Islands, came to an end about 1270 B.C. It appears their villages were abandoned when they were threatened by the warlike Sikels, Ausonians and Morgeti from the Italian Mainland. Most of the Thapsos people took refuge in Pantalica, in the rough interior of Sicily.[12] However, having known and traded with the people of Borg in-Nadur, it also seems possible that some of them should have taken refuge in Malta instead.

The third possibility is the Milazzese culture of Panarea in the Aeolian Islands. In about 1250 B.C., the same invaders from the Italian Mainland sacked their villages,[13] and their people were driven out. Like the people of Lipari, there is no

---

[6] Brea, 1966, p. 109.
[7] Margaret Guido, "Sicily: An archaeological Guide", 1967, pp. 38–9 (hereafter Guido, 1967).
[8] Brea, 1966, p. 110.
[9] Brea, 1966, p. 132.
[10] Evans, Blue Guide—Malta, 1968, p. 21.
[11] Trump, 23.2.75.
[12] Guido, 1967, pp. 197, 192.
[13] Guido, 1967, pp. 38, 39

knowledge of where these people may have taken refuge.[14] However, having possibly been related to the people of the older Capo Graziano culture of Lipari, and being of a contemporary culture with those of the Thapsos villages, the people of Panarea may also have chosen to take refuge in Malta.

If, as appears possible, the Borg in-Nadur people came from the Aeolian Islands and Sicily, it would follow that, while they had developed a new culture, they were all related to the Tarxien Cemetery people and therefore were also principally Dinaric. This would account, as Dr. Trump states, for the persistence of the characteristics of that Caucasoid subracial type with a long face and round, often flattened, head "which survives to the present day, unaffected by later and lesser immigrations".[15]

As was noted with respect to the Tarxien Cemetery people who cremated their dead while their counterpart in Sicily buried theirs, this contradiction also existed between the Borg in-Nadur and their possible antecedents in Sicily and the Aeolian Islands. However, such a difference still had little significance as shown by Milazzo in Sicily where a cemetery was found of the Millazzese phase, containing about 50 burials crouched in huge vases, but in which the burials had later (1150–1050 B.C.) been placed in urns.[16]

Borg in-Nadur pottery suggests a decline in this culture during the long period until it was superseded by the Phoenician/Punic.[17]

In about 1000 B.C.,[18] a new wave of immigrants occurred. According to the types of pottery they produced, they appear to have been of the Fossa-Grave Culture of Campania and Calabria in southern Italy, specifically the cemetery of Canala Janchina where similar types of pottery were found.[19] However, the pottery they produced in Malta was clearly derived from that of the Middle Bronze Age (Borg in-Nadur) people while that of the Middle Bronze Age people also continued in use.

The new immigrants settled on a defendable plateau, Il-Qleigha, in the Bahrija area, after which they were named locally, joining the Middle Bronze Age people who continued to live side by side with them. Although the plateau is bordered on the west and north by high cliffs, it was more suitable as a settlement than most of the others occupied by Bronze Age peoples, as it was bordered by a slope of cultivable fields on the east and the valley below could be reached more easily than was the case with other settlement sites. From the widespread scattering of sherds, some of which bear attractive, minute designs by these Late

[14] Brea, 10.8.76.
[15] Trump, 1966, p. 49.
[16] Guido, 1967, pp. 38–9.
[17] Trump, 1966, p. 44.
[18] Trump, 23.2.75.
[19] Trump, 1966, p. 50.

Bronze Age people, it appears that the plateau was occupied throughout by a village. There are no remains of huts but an L shaped wall extending out from the high part of the main rubble wall running down the centre of the plateau, may be from this period.

Excavations by Dr. D. H. Trump in 1959, brought forth a surprising number of bronze objects, which indicate that a frequent exchange of goods with other areas in the Mediterranean was maintained. Among the finds were clay spindle-whorls, loom weights and anchor shaped pieces of pottery which may have served as part of a loom. One loom weight, which is of exceptional size and de-corated with an incised pattern resembling that of Late Bronze Age pottery, parallels those found in contemporary sites in Sicily and southwest Italy.[20] These finds indicate that the weaving industry of these people had reached proportions of considerable importance, and accounted largely for the exports made in return for the bronze objects noted above. In fact, the first records appear from this time of the high reputation Maltese textiles had gained in overseas areas.[21]

DEFENCE WALLS

The Early Bronze Age people appear to have settled largely on the ridges above the southwest coast of Malta and at Ta' Cenc in Gozo. At Wied Maqbul, just west of Hal Far, there are three barren plateaux, one below the other, extending out to the edge of the cliff. On the lowest of these is what appears to be a defence wall made of large, flat upright stones with a circular enclosed area at the east end; up above to the south toward the cliff is another small circular enclosed area (544636). When excavated, the enclosed area at the end of the wall, was heaped with a small rhomboidal "cairn" of stones.[22] Another Early/Middle Bronze Age settle-ment appears to have been at Wardija ta' Zuta (464668) where at the apex of the rocky ridge there are rows of fairly large stones that might have been defence walls, as well as a village; there is also one large, flat stone raised at one end by stones, which might have been a dolmen, and leading out to the west from them are several pairs of cart-ruts.

On the barren ridge at Ta' Cenc, south of Sannat, there are, in addition to several dolmens, a group of dilapidated remains at Id-Dura Tax-Xaghra II-Kbira. They appear to have composed two parallel lines of stone uprights. These might have been defence walls or, as Dr. Trump states, they may have been a ruined gallery grave of the type found in the Bari region of south-east Italy.[23]

[20] Evans, 1971, pp. 105, 227–8.
[21] Trump, 1972, pp. 104–5.
[22] Evans, 1971, p. 193.
[23] Evans, 1971, p. 198.

About 100 yards up the ridge from their settlement on Borg in-Nadur, the Middle Bronze Age people built a large defence wall. It is from this "Fortress on the Hill" that the name of the ridge in Maltese was derived. It is 13′ 6″ high and 5′ thick, and runs across the neck of the ridge. It is in the shape of a capital D, the flat side of which was about 180′ across on the outside and 110′ on the inside. The radius of the half circle was about 44′.[24] A large part of the outside of the curved wall is still of the original large stones measuring 7′ 4″ × 2′ 4″ × 2′, but on the inside it has been mostly restored as has the straight wall. Strangely enough the straight wall of the fort faced the settlement while the curved wall faces up the ridge indicating that the enemy was expected to come from down the ridge rather than the end of the ridge, which slopes down to the bay, where, no doubt, the real danger from invasion from overseas existed. On the numerous other ridges on which the Middle Bronze Age people settled, it appears that they selected sites at their ends, just inside the cliffs, where no intruder could have approached, and placed their defence walls a few feet out from them. Running down from the back of the defence wall at Borg in-Nadur was an extension on the east side; it measured 88′ straight down toward the south and then curved out to the east for another 65′. A corresponding wall presumably also ran down to the south from the west side and then curved gradually out to the west.

Alongside the Borg in-Nadur village running up the west side of the ridge from Nadur Street at Birzebbuga is a broad promenade of levelled limestone about 10′ to 15′ wide. It does not appear to have been caused naturally but rather was made by the Middle Bronze Age people who lived there. Such a wide, smooth strip of stone also borders the cliff running east and west of Wied Mixta along the south coast of Malta. The cliff has fallen away in places and the smooth strip of stone is missing at such places, but the possibility suggests itself that this was also a promenade made by Middle Bronze Age people who lived in the caves there.

DOLMENS

The dolmen, which comes from an outcrop of coralline limestone which has fissured into loose blocks a foot or more thick and about 10′ by 5′, was used as the capstone over two uprights at the ends, like the trilithon in a Copper Age temple, but only 1′ to 3′ above the ground. Below it, an urn containing the ashes, probably of some leader, was placed. As the coralline limestone shows little effect from the weather, the dolmens appear, when left in their natural state, much as they did originally. Two dozen or more have been identified in Malta and Gozo, but as some of them have been used in a farm wall (such as that at Ta′ Zuta) or for low sheds, only those described below are easy to find and worth visiting.

[24] Evans, 1971, p. 14 and Plan 2.

Il-Bidni (599695)

A narrow paved road, which branches off the main road to Marsascala from Zabbar at bus stop 7, goes up the hill diagonally to Tad-Dawl chapel. It continues on to the left past the chapel and comes after about 100 yards, to an opening in the rubble wall to the left. Diagonally back across the field there in a north-easterly direction is an opening in another rubble wall, and beyond that diagonally down to the right about 200 feet is the dolmen.

The capstone is 8' × 5' 10'', and it has an average thickness of 1'. It is supported on three sides by stone blocks and is open on one short side. It was pierced by a hole about 5'' in diameter, which weakened it, so that it split in two, but has not fallen down at all.

Wied Znuber (559634)

At the head of the ravine of Wied Znuber, enclosed by a wall and located within the area of the Hal Far Airfield is a most interesting dolmen (figure 13).

13. Wied Znuber Dolmen

Its capstone is 12' 4'' × 5' 4''. The top of it has a recess in it measuring 3' 6'' × 2' 2'' and 2'' deep. There are six hollows, one at each corner, and one at the edge in the middle of each long side. There is also a groove across one end of the slab. These marks may well be contemporary as they appear on various dolmens but as they often also have been made into the top of tall stones and elsewhere to attract birds to rain water collected there, they may be more or less modern. Below the capstone, the live rock has been hollowed out; the chamber there measures up to 28'' in height, on each side of which is a block 1' high.

Wied Filep (488754)

There are two dolmens at this site which is in a field, surrounded by a rubble wall, about 200 feet off the old Mosta-Naxxar road, at a turn just south of the quarry. One dolmen has been tilted up by a stone which was inserted apparently to get at the grave below but not subsequently removed. Its capstone is 11' 10'' × 5' 6'' and 2' thick. It is supported on either end by stones about 4' high.

A few feet away, the second dolmen is lying a few inches above the ground with one side on the edge of a low rock and the other on small stones. Its capstone is 10' × 5' to 6' 6''.

Ta' Hammut (501779)

In the valley of Il-Maghtab, about two-tenths of a mile up a paved road from the coast road at Qalet Marku are three dolmens in a field about 120' to the right. The first is a slab 8' × 4' × 22'' resting on boulders some 20'' above the live rock which had been hollowed out in the centre to form a recess in which the urn containing the ashes of the deceased was probably placed. When excavated in 1955, a number of sherds were found, all of which were of the normal Tarxien Cemetery type. Nearby is another oval depression over which a dolmen may also have been placed.

About 100' beyond and about the same distance from the road, is the second dolmen standing on the bare, live rock. A step in the rock surface has been used to increase the height of the chamber below the capstone, which is 5' 8'' × 4' 2'' and 14'' thick. It is supported on either side by slabs, resting on irregular blocks in front of the step in the live rock.

A third dolmen, some 100' farther on in a straight line has been built into a bird shooting blind. Its capstone is 7' 2'' × 3' 11'' and is 1' 10'' thick.

Ta' Sansuna (335903)

Said to be probably a collapsed dolmen,[25] this would be the granddaddy of them all. It measures 21' 6'' by 18' and is about 3' 6'' thick; the right end measuring 6' 6'' in length is broken and leans down. It is raised on a stone 2–3 feet high on the left and one somewhat lower on the right. It is estimated that it weighs from 35 to 40 tons. It is located in a walled in area on the left side of the road which is marked with signs to the Cornucopia Hotel at Xaghra. As it is well above the ravine and no other large stones are found near, it seems it must have been brought there by a man or better a woman; according to legend, a giantess with a baby in a cradle on her back carried it there on her head and she held the supporting stones in either hand.

Ta' Cenc (529869)

On the left side of the main road going down to Ta' Cenc from Sannat in Gozo is a string of what appears to be 20 dolmens, which either had been completed

---

[25] Trump, 1972, p. 158.

of were in a state of preparation; it being difficult from their present state of preservation to determine, only three can be said definitely to be dolmens. There are also two places on the right of the road near the compound of the hotel which appear to have been dolmens.

Id-Dura Tal-Mara (532866)

Down the Ta' Cenc plateau and out to the right near the ruins of the Copper Age temple, Il-Borg ta' L-Imramma, is a dolmen whose capstone measures 9' 7" × 6' and 1' 6" thick. It rests on several uprights, one of which is 3' high.

SILOS

At St. George's Bay, opposite Pinto's Battery, where a side street runs up the hill to the ruins of the megalithic temple on Borg in-Nadur, it appears that some 3,500 years ago, the edge of the bay must have been located a considerable distance from where it is now and that the level of the sea was possibly as much as 10' below what is at present. A general sinking of the whole southeast corner of Malta seems to have taken place gradually over several hundred thousand years or more, while the northwest corner of the island at Dingli and beyond has been tilted upward. This is indicated by the presence of some dozen silo pits about 3' 6" in diameter and about 5' deep, which were cut into the rock by the side of the road and now washed over by the sea. These silos, like those else-where on the islands, have been identified through the sherds found in them as being the products of the Middle Bronze Age, but they were also made by the Late Bronze Age people and possibly those of the Early Bronze Age as well. Those at the side of St. George's Bay were probably used for storing grain and/or olive oil; their location by the edge of the bay was probably selected to afford better access for the boats loading there. There are also two pairs of cart-ruts at that point, at right angles to one another, which were probably used for transporting the grain or oil to and from the silos there. However, the sinking of the coast at some time in the past, possibly 2,500 years ago, must have rendered the cart-ruts no longer usable, as they then ran into the bay on both sides of the point while the silos remained fairly well above the sea level. What is remarkable is that when it became necessary to abandon the cart-ruts, an additional number of silos were cut into the live rock between their former tracks.

Silo pits have been found in a number of other places on both Malta and Gozo. There are about a dozen of them on Il-Qlejgha plateau at Bahrija, some of which are connected by passages near the top, as well as on the table mountain of Nuffara opposite Ggantija Temple in Gozo. They have been observed also at Wardija ta' Zuta on the west coast of Malta (464668) where there was a walled village, apparently a dolmen, and cart-ruts running out from the area (which may have been an Early/Middle Bronze Age settlement), and at Qala Hill above San Martin in Malta. In addition, groups of much larger silos have been found at the Citadel in Gozo and on Mtarfa Ridge in Malta.

It was reported at the end of last century,[26] that about 100 bell-shaped silos were still lying beyond the line of fortifications in the Salito del Gran Castello at Gozo. They were cut into the rock to form several rows underlying one another and communicating by vertical and horizontal passages. They had been made, according to local information, for use in storing supplies. According to an illustration, they were 6' in diameter and 8' high and had a bottle-neck opening of about 18" and the same width for the passages connecting them It was also reported that ten similar bell-shaped silos were discovered at Mtarfa near the military barracks in 1892. They were in a row and connected by passages. They measured 10' by 10' and their bottle-neck like openings and passages were likewise 18" in diameter. In 1939, two bell-shaped silos were investigated near the married quarters of the Mtarfa Barracks.[27] One was about 14' deep and had a narrow bottle-neck mouth; Late Bronze Age cinerary urns were found at the bottom of the pit, which apparently had been placed there for temporary storage and forgotten. The second silo had been cut down and used as a tomb in Punic times.

CART-RUTS

Cart-ruts have been observed in Sicily, Sardinia and Cyrenaica in the Mediterranean, and in some places elsewhere. On Malta, they are probably the most numerous; they are found in almost every part of the rural areas, and they appear in several parts of Gozo as well. These cart-ruts appear today just as they did some thousands of years ago, as the hard coralline limestone into which they are worn has not perceptibly eroded. Parallel ruts, varying from 52 to 58 inches apart, skirt the rocky terrain and are a notable characteristic of the landscape. The cart-ruts themselves are often 8 to 12 inches or more in width and usually V shaped with a narrow groove at the base no wider than the lower joint of a man's thumb, and slightly concave, while others are U shaped and without a groove. Some have been filled in with soil, appearing as stripes of grass trailing across the bare surface of ridges and plateaux, and sometimes crossing like railway switches. Some are worn deep into the rock, up to 2' or more, and in winter and spring may be used by the farmers as small reservoirs.

They are familiar to the Maltese and the visitor alike but to all they are an enigma. A number of eminent archaeologists have made extensive studies of

[26] A. A. Caruana, 1898, "Ancient Pagan Tombs and Christian Cemeteries", p. 75.
[27] Evans, 1971, p. 107.

them but as, apart from the cart-ruts themselves, there had been no real evidence to go on, they remained as much a mystery as ever. Who made them, when, where did they go, what caused them, for what purpose, and if made by a cart, what animal pulled it, how was it constructed, and was it on wheels or runners? These are the questions that are often asked.

Because Punic tombs have often been found cut into them, archaeologists have assumed that the Middle Bronze Age people had made them and, of course, the Late Bronze Age people would likewise have been responsible for some of them. However, it appears that the Early Bronze Age people may have been responsible for them originally, such as at Wardija ta' Zuta and Ta' Cenc, Gozo, where there are dolmens.

As for the last date the cart-ruts may have been used, this appears to have varied greatly. Some, such as those at St. George's Bay, where silos were cut into their paths, were obviously abandoned even during the Middle/Late Bronze Age. Some, moreover, had Punic tombs cut into them, possibly even before the arrival of the Carthaginians in 600 B.C. On the other hand, there are reasons to believe that many may have continued in use even up into Roman times. From observing the terrain and the limited number of roads where even the high wheeled farm carts could have driven over the rocky ridges and promontories, it appears that the inhabitants may have found it more practical to use them as long as they remained there. This possibly lasted in some areas until those living there were brought down to Melita and the Gozo Citadel, which had been walled by the Romans for their safety; this may not have been accomplished finally until the end of the first century A.D.

Cart-ruts appear in all kinds of places, even running off cliffs and into the sea. However, most of them do show a general pattern connecting the sites of former Bronze Age settlements, which are perched often one after the other on a series of ridges, and apparently covered long distances up and down the island. For example, there is a large group of cart-ruts at the edge of the ridge at Mtarfa; they have been traced up to the side of the road at Nadur Hill and again on to Bingemma Gap. Another group is to the east of Falka Gap on the fault of Victoria Lines; they have been traced to a further group on the ridge below, then half way up Bidnija Ridge and finally to a group of cart-ruts on top. A similar pattern is found at Naxxar Gap, where there must have been a particularly large settlement; these have been traced to the ravine below and then to the top of Mosta Fort; and half way down the slope below Naxxar Gap, two pairs make a graceful curve back and then become lost but apparently went to Salina Bay. At the end of the bay are some of the deepest cart-ruts on the island and it has been suggested that heavy loads of salt were brought up from there on the carts that made the ruts.

As for the cart-ruts that run off cliffs, they may be explained by the fact that a part of the area has fallen into the sea at sometime since they were made. Those

60

that run into the sea, such as two pairs running into St. George's Bay at Birzeb-buga, are, as previously explained, due to the tilting of the island downward to the southeast by possibly 10' during the past 3,500 years.

As the average width between the centre grooves of the cart-ruts is consistently about 55", it appears, as the name implies, that they must have been made by a cart of some kind, although initially, they may have been cut a bit by hand in order to direct the cart on a specific route. In many places where the cart-ruts disappear for long or short distances, it is assumed that the carts had traversed a deposit of earth which then covered the surface of the rock. On the other hand, terraces have been built up to form fields for cultivation and covered over the cart-ruts that may have been there.

From the general pattern of cart-ruts running between former Bronze Age settlements, it appears there must have been a tremendous amount of traffic between them, transporting goods, possibly soil or anything. This would account in addition for the considerable depth and width of the cart-ruts in some places. The patterns of switches, and marshaling yards found at former Bronze Age settlements suggest, moreover, that there must have been many carts as well as a lot of coming and going.

At "Clapham Junction", a former Bronze Age settlement, which is on a slope above Buskett, the cart-ruts are particularly numerous and, unlike those elsewhere, several cross one another at right angles. This suggests that they might have been used for ceremonial purposes, possibly decorated festively, such as the funeral carts in Bali that, with flying, long banners are pulled slowly across the fields.

It is usually thought that these carts had been pulled by a draft animal but there are no tracks, except where the ruts indicate they were used in more recent times by wagons. There are in some places, however, small grooves cut between the ruts which served to keep the animal that pulled the cart from slipping. Such grooves are often found on foot paths where men, ancient or modern, made them for themselves. One is lead to believe, therefore, that the animal in question was man, or more likely two men, who, each with an arm over the shoulder of the other, could make a powerful team, capable of pulling a loaded cart up the steep slopes on the sides of the ridges and plateaux. Except for the grooves, which are found usually where there is a steep decline, the surface between the cart-ruts is generally smooth and may indicate the wear of bare feet but, due to the slight weathering of the hard coralline limestone, would no longer show any sign of such wear. That men may have pulled the carts is suggested also by a pair of cart-ruts that lead into a cave which has such a low entrance that only men, bending way down, could have entered pulling the cart after them.

The cart in question is generally assumed to have been similar to that used by the Red Indians of America, namely, with a shaft or pole on either side and a platform half way back. With men pulling the cart, however, there also would have been a brace across the front against which they could push.

A test was made a few years ago for the B.B.C. to determine whether such a cart might have had wheels. Due to the depth of the cart-ruts, however, it was found that a wheel could not have been used as it would have become stuck at the curves. Consequently, it was reasoned that the end of the shafts must have been shod with a stone runner especially as the shaft would have been worn down in no time had it come into direct contact with the stone surface, and, moreover, would never have worn a rut. However, no evidence had been uncovered that would substantiate that assumption.

The breakthrough came in 1974 when excavating Punic tombs at a Bronze Age settlement site which is crisscrossed with cart-ruts. One of the excavators came upon a peculiarly shaped stone, which was obviously shaped by man, and appeared to be designed in such a way that it could be wedged into the split end of a wooden shaft and held with a copper band or a leather thong. Another stone, similar to the first, was soon found by the cart-ruts, which is in the shape of a shoe and distinctly worn where a band or thong might have been placed to keep it wedged into the end of a shaft. About a dozen more stones, which could have served as runners, were found, all of which were of coralline or some other hard stone brought in from abroad.

It was noted that all of these stones would have fitted into the basic concave groove of the cart-ruts, that their under surface is slightly convex, and that in all of them, it was worn at about the same angle, i.e., 5 degrees. This angle indicated that the shafts had not been parallel but had pointed somewhat inward. Some of the stones showed, moreover, that they had been wedged into the shaft in such a way that the shafts would have been held up about 4' when the cart was being drawn (figure 14).

With this evidence, it was possible to determine what the cart was like. This was done first by taking the average width of 55" between the grooves of the cart-ruts as the distance between the two stone runners. Then it was assumed that the brace across the front must be about 40" to allow room for two men side by side. Then, taking the angle of 5 degrees on the under surface of the stone runners, a mathematical formula was used to determine the length between the stone runner and the brace; it was 82.87".

With the length of the shaft between the stone runner and the brace being approximately 83", the width of the brace where it meets the shaft being 3", and leaving 1' as a hand hold, the total length of the shaft would be 8' 2".

Using the above measurements, a cart was constructed. In order to carry a heavy load, the shafts were made quite thick, i.e., 2" × 2½". And to have them quite stiff, so that they should follow the grooves, although the pressure of the load would cause the shafts to spread a bit, they were made of ash, a wood that

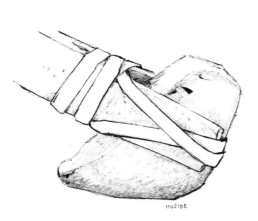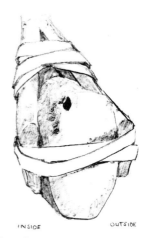

INSIDE   INSIDE   OUTSIDE

14. Stone Runner that Made the Cart-Ruts

grew in Malta in the Bronze Age it is understood. Finally, a platform, made of three thick, straight limbs, was placed half way between the brace and the rear end of the shafts, and notched to keep the shafts from spreading.

In order to insert the stone runners, which are about 4″ long and $1\frac{1}{4}″$ wide, into the shafts, a rectangular hole about $\frac{5}{8}″ \times 2″$ was made into them and the top part of the stones, one of which had served apparently as a runner originally, was cut accordingly.

The cart, loaded with a burden of over 200 pounds, has been tested several times in the cart-ruts both at Naxxar Gap and Mtarfa. Those on the slope below Naxxar Gap afforded an exacting test as they are deep and narrow and curve back and forth down the hill. Holding the brace above the belt and thus reducing the angle of the shafts at the top of the ruts to a minimum, the cart sought out the grooves in the ruts without difficulty, and only at times came slightly in contact with the inner sides of the ruts. The stone runners glided smoothly over the stone surface and only slightly furrowed the soil that covered the ruts in places.

Having proved that the cart could easily run within the existing cart-ruts, there remained the question whether it would actually make the ruts in time. This seemed to be answered by the abrasion of the surface of the groove at the bottom of the cart-ruts, which had been caused by the runners while the latter showed little wear. That the cart would eventually cut out a wide V or U rut was indicated, moreover, by the fact that the two shafts moved uniformly in jerks from side to side when not locked in the basic groove of the cart-ruts.

Thus, it appears that a cart with shafts resting on stone runners at the ends could have been the vehicle in the Bronze Age that made the cart-ruts. That

63

it was such a cart appears to be indicated by the shape of a number of stones, found lying about at former Bronze Age settlements where there are cart-ruts, which appear to have been made by man and seem to fit the requirements of runners when tested in various cart-ruts. These stone runners, moreover, not only served as models for those used in the test cart but also afforded the basic measurement for the construction of the cart which proved to be both simple and practical for use on the rocky surface of the ridges and ravines of Malta and Gozo.

CHAPTER V

SANCTUARIES

The sanctuaries were the cultural focus of life on Malta and Gozo from the time the Phoenicians established trading centres on the Islands in 850 B.C., on through the Carthaginian occupation from 600 to 218 B.C., and up into the I century A.D. under Roman rule. As such, they were the fulcrum by which the native Bronze Age population was assimilated under Phoenician–Punic influence and which the Romans later adopted as their own, while a native, neo-Punic cultural variant developed and came to dominate the life of the country.

That the reception of the Phoenicians by the Bronze Age population was friendly and cooperative is borne out by the evidence afforded by archaeological finds at their native sites. Dr. D. H. Trump stated, with respect to both Borg in-Nadur and Bahrija pottery types, that they were all rapidly superseded by imported Phoenician pottery and that there is little evidence of there having been a period between them when they overlapped. Receiving Phoenician pottery and having an important export product in their textiles that were already highly prized by other peoples in the Mediterranean (Diodorus referred to Malta's women's clothes, remarkably fine, and soft hats and cushions), it would naturally follow that they welcomed the Phoenicians as middlemen on the islands.

Ptolemy wrote that the Phoenicians did not limit themselves to the harbours but occupied the interior as well and presumably founded Melita (present Rabat–Mdina). Dr. D. H. Trump further pointed out that Phoenician control, as shown by their tombs in Rabat, Nigret (Rabat area), Mtarfa, Siggiewi, and Paola, had spread over the whole island.[1] In addition, he noted with respect to cultural sequences, that the Middle Bronze Age people had continued alongside the Late Bronze Age until both disappeared under Phoenician influence.[2]

[1] Trump, 1972, p. 23.
[2] Trump, 1966, p. 20.

Prof. Cagiano de Azevedo believes there was very little intermarriage between the Phoenicians, or the Carthaginians who followed them, with the native Bronze Age people.[3] What appears to have been important, as shown by their respective pottery types found during excavations as Tas Silg, where the the Phoenicians established a sanctuary possibly already in the VIII century B.C., was that they must have lived alongside one another during the IX to VIII centuries B.C. at the site of the proto-historical temple still standing there.[4]

During the VII to VI centuries B.C., the Phoenicians took over the temple and included it in their sanctuary to the Goddess Astarte, constructed a passage in front of it, and inserted walls in front of its entrance, while the area adjoining the temple to the northwest was rearranged.[4]

Under the Phoenicians, the population of Malta must have grown quite large if, as Stephan of Byzantium wrote, the Maltese had founded a colony at Acholla, opposite Malta on the eastern coast of Tunisia. This colony must have been established before the Carthaginians took over, as it appears it was not attacked during the Punic Wars, and has continued until now as the modern town of Botria.

When the Phoenicians in Tyre and Sidon were defeated by the Assyrians and Babylonians in about 600 B.C., the Carthaginians took over Malta and other Phoenician colonies in the Western and Central Mediterranean. Malta became a strategic stronghold to prevent the Greeks in Sicily from expanding to the south.[5]

It should be mentioned at this point that Greece never had a colony in Malta, notwithstanding such indications by classical writers, such as Ovid's Fasti (III, 565ff) that it had. He wrote "There is a fertile island Melita, lashed by the waves of the Lybian Sea, and neighbour to the barren Cosyra (Pantelleria). Anna steared for it, trusting to the King's hospitality which she had known of old, for Battus there was king, a wealthy host . .3" However, it appears that Anna, sister of Elissa who founded Carthage in 814 B.C., escaped from there a few years later and went to Italy, and could not have found Battus in Malta as he, who was a Greek, lived some 170 later and is known to have followed the advice of the oracle in Delphi and established a colony in Cyrene in North Africa in 630 B.C.[6]

The Carthaginians were apparently quite numerous, although possibly made up to a large extent of soldiers and officials. They may have also included,

[3] Interview 28.II.75.

[4] "Missione Archeologica a Malta", 1964–70.

[5] Trump, 1972, p. 23.

[6] Classical Dictionary, by J. Lempriere originally, 1958, pp. 48, 104.

however, some Libyphoenicians as, according to classical sources, they had done in their colonies in Spain.[7]

All citizens of Malta, as in other Carthaginian colonies in the Mediterranean, were never regarded as Carthaginian but were allowed a limited form of Government of their own.[8] A Maltese inscription cites a Government system including suffetes, senate and people, in the same form as that for the Carthaginians. Malta and Gozo, moreover, were permitted to mint their own coins. On the other hand, Carthage subjugated them, and exploited them, especially their textile industry, but it never sought to integrate them into a large, unitary community with itself.[9] Like other Carthaginian colonies, Malta was not an open market, it was reserved to the Carthaginians as it was possible to avoid all competition there, and to ensure navigation, Carthage protected its cities and maritime posts against piracy.[10]

During the V century, it appears that the Punics in Malta, as in Carthage, turned in on themselves; there was a strong reaction against all foreigners, especially Greek influence, which had become strong. The power of the priesthood, reinforced by refugees from Tyre, seems to have increased in influence and, as in Carthage, may have caused those in Malta to have become restrained in their outlook, conservative and obstinate, while yet remaining capable, both as a people and as individuals of great courage and nobility.[11]

As a result, the artistic production of the Punics in Malta appears to have degenerated during this period as it did in Carthage. According to Gsell,[12] "The technique degenerated after the fifth century. We can attribute the poor quality of their jewels to a wish to curb expenditure which was deemed useless. . . . The truth was that the Punic craftsmen no longer took the trouble to work well; they left that to the Greeks. They performed their daily task without enjoying it. There was a great demand for cheap objects, while the commercial monopolies almost put the buyer at the mercy of the seller. . . . The artistic talents of a nation appear in the commonest objects and these prove the hopeless incapacity of the Carthaginians who were not even able to imitate their Greek model".

Following the decline of Greek influence from the V to the end of the IV century B.C., Malta, like Carthage, apparently again came under the influence of Hellenism as a result of Carthage's coming back into the mainstream of Mediterranean civilization. The war in 310–307 B.C., when the neighbouring town of

[7] Sabatino Moscati, "The World of the Phoenicians", 1968, p. 288, (hereafter, Moscati, 1968).

[8] Moscati, 1968, p. 170.

[9] Moscati, 1968, p. 174.

[10] S. Gsell, IV, "Histoire Ancienne L'Afrique", p. 113, (hereafter, Gsell, IV).

[11] Susan Raven, "Rome in Africia", 1969, p. 12, (hereafter, Raven, 1969).

[12] S. Gsell, IV, pp. 107–8.

Utica was pillaged by the Greeks, made it clear to Carthage that it was not impregnable and that it must seek alliances where it could, such as the Hellenistic state of Egypt.[13] Greek prisoners of war in Sicily were brought back as slaves to Carthage and presumably to Malta as well where they introduced Greek skills in sculpture, etc.

The cultural changes during the V, IV and III centuries B.C. appear to have been reflected in the development of the sanctuary at Tas Silg, where there was no further construction during the V century, while in the IV, it was limited to building a courtyard. In the III century B.C., however, Hellenistic architecture was incorporated in the construction of the sanctuary, when various additions were made including the building of a porch. Also there was a Hellenistic influence in the construction of the sanctuary at Ras il-Wardija in Gozo, which was established in the III century B.C. In addition, both sanctuaries became dedicated to the Greek Goddess Hera as well as to Astarte-Tanit.[14]

Although Hellenistic influences prevailed during this time, it appears that in Malta, as in Carthage, there was probably no sign of the humanism of the Greek world. The elaborate religious ceremonies were the only public functions while the theatre was unknown. There were no games and no athletes. Plutarch wrote that the Carthaginians, which might have been said of the Punics in Malta as well, were: "a hard and gloomy people, submissive to their rulers and harsh to their subjects; they kept obstinately to their decisions, were austere and cared little for amusement or the graces of life".[15]

In 256 B.C., Malta was laid waste during the First Punic War by the army of Atilius Regulus, who disembarked there en route to Africa, and although re-occupied by the Carthaginians, it fell to the Romans thirty odd years later at the beginning of the Second Punic War in 218 B.C. It appears it was simply that the Punic force, left without a fleet, was too small to defend itself, and there is no reason to suppose that the local population, which themselves had become thoroughly Punic in their beliefs, customs and manners, had rebelled[16] Livy, the consul, wrote in 218 B.C., with respect to the fall of Punic Malta to the Romans: "sailed for Malta, which was in Carthaginian hands; Hamilcar, the son of Gisgo, commander of the island's garrison, surrendered with nearly 2,000 men, and the island and the town passed into Roman control".[17]

Upon occupying Malta without resistance, the Romans had no cause to take vengeance upon the population as was the custom elsewhere in the Empire,

[13] Moscati, 1968, p. 147.
[14] "Missione Archeologica a Malta", 1964–70.
[15] Susan Raven, 1969, p. 20.
[16] Moscati, 1968, p. 190
[17] Livy, "The War with Hannibal", Book XXI, paragraph 51, Penguin Classics.

nor, in view of its small size, did they make any attempt to colonize it. Having made the Empire secure in the middle Mediterranean through the defeat of Carthage, Malta had no strategic significance and thus required only a small garrison. Malta and Gozo were declared confederates and allies of the Roman people, which implies they had autonomous governments with the right of sending Legates to the Roman Senate, and both Islands were allowed to mint their own coins. To maintain and administer them during the confused and strife ridden period of the Republic in Rome, there was little that it could do but to place them under a propraetor in Sicily.

The sanctuaries and their important place in the religious life of both the Romans and the native population, however, served to bring them together. The Romans accepted the Goddess Astarte as their own while the neo-Punic natives welcomed the Roman Gods, identifying Tanit with Juno, Baal with Saturn and Melcart with Hercules. As recent excavations have shown, the enlargement of the sanctuary at Tas Silg continued under the Romans, while that at Ras il-Wardija in Gozo experienced a transition from the influence of Carthage to that of Rome.

It is recorded that an admiral of King Masinissa of Numidia (c. 238–149 B.C.) landed in Malta and plundered the ancient and famous sanctuary of Juno, which "stood on a promontory close to the town, taking from there certain elephants' tusks of enormous size, but that the king sent them back, carved with Punic inscriptions, stating that he had done so". The town here referred to, evidently confirms a local tradition that one had existed at the site of Tas Silg. There is also a tradition that one likewise existed on the promontory of Wardija, adjoining the sanctuary at Tanit-Hera-Juno at Ras il-Wardija in Gozo.

In 71 B.C., Verres, the propraetor in Sicily, organized a systematic pillaging of his province, including Malta, taking away the treasures of the sanctuary of Juno, among which were the same elephants' tusks. Cicero, who prosecuted Verres, described specifically his depradations, and paid tribute to this sanctuary, saying that it and one at Samos, on an island west of Anatolia, were the oldest in the Mediterranean. Verres was reported also to have destroyed the temple to Proserpine, the Goddess of the underworld, which apparently existed at Mtarfa, the hill to the north of Melita; an imperial inscription now in the Roman Museum at Rabat, records the governor of the islands, one Chrestion, Aug (usti) lib(ertus), proc(urator) insularum Melit. et Gaul, restored it.

According to the evidence found in the excavations of both the sanctuaries at Tas-Silg and Ras il-Wardija, they became slowly abandoned during the I century A.D.,[18] as apparently life became centred in Melita and Gaulus, and those in the cities adjoining them were withdrawn within the walls of the Roman cities.

[18] "Missione Archeologica a Malta", 1963–70.

In addition to the sanctuaries at Tas Silg and Ras il-Wardija and the temple to Proserpine on Mtarfa, it appears there might have been one at Ghajn Rihana Valley on a terrace below Gebel Ghawzara on the Bidnija Ridge in Malta, and from the mixture of Punic and Roman sherds to be found on some fields at Ceqqufija, meaning in Maltese "a lot of pottery", just to the north of San Lawrenz in Gozo, there may have been a sanctuary there as well.

TAS SILG

The Copper Age temple at Tas Silg (see Megalithic Temples) was still standing and in use in the IX–VIII centuries B.C. by the Bronze Age peoples. It was incorporated into a sanctuary to Astarte, the Goddess of fertility, beauty and love, established by the Phoenicians in the VIII–VII century B.C., maintained and improved by the Carthaginians and the native population until the occupation of the islands by the Romans in 218 B.C., then adopted by the Romans as the temple to Juno and attended and supported by the neo-Punic natives until some time during the I century A.D.[18]

The crescent, extending out from the Copper Age temple on either side to the north, was rearranged during the VII and VI centuries B.C., and during the IV and III centuries B.C., the temple was incorporated into the Punic sanctuary by joining its interior to a vast courtyard opening before it. A semicircular wall before the temple linked the two. A portico was installed as a transition from one shape to another. Consequently, it was possible to distribute all the quadrangular rooms opening onto the courtyard along orthogonal axes, to form a functional sanctuary that would satisfy the needs of the Punics. In addition, the temple was refurbished and a large door was cut into the crescent shaped facade. As a result, the sanctuary became similar to other Punic sanctuaries of that period. Punic culture, in fact, seems to have been somewhat detached from Carthage, while the tie to the Phoenicians was stronger.

It is noteworthy that the religious life of the site from its inception in the Copper Age up to Phoenician-Punic times and then the Roman was dedicated to a feminine divinity. First, was the obese Mother Goddess of the Copper Age temple. The next was Astarte of the Phoenicians, followed by Astarte-Tanit of the Punics. Under the influence of the Hellenistic culture, Punic religious rites and practices were changed and dedications in Greek to Hera were found. Dedications to Hera, as well as to Juno, also appeared in the Roman period. While meeting the different needs at different times, however, the sanctuary retained the same characteristics throughout its long existence.

The sanctuary was rich in works of art and votive offerings from the time of its inception.

During Punic times, the sanctuary incorporated structures of the Hellenistic

70

period and the plan of the buildings resembled that of the Hellenistic period, but they were all arranged in a perfectly orthogonol distribution with the intent to incorporate and honour that "perfect gem", the Copper Age temple.

The installations of the neo-Punics, which were carried out in the II and I centuries B.C., must have been large and sumptuous; there were elegant architectural structures, built with great care and expertness, with fine floors of slabs of stone and elegant mosaics and architectural decorations applied on the walls. The ornamentation of the sanctuary was rich throughout. The collection of votive offerings (pots of cosmetics, hairpins, pearls, ear-rings, rings etc.) were apparently made by women. There were also many imports of highly artistic objects, including marble statues, all of which represented women. There were also many murex shells, indicating that the women were occupied in dyeing textiles like their Phoenician predecessors.

During the Roman period, I century B.C. to I century A.D., they constructed a great portico with a columned passage, paved with brick and marble mosaics, a courtyard paved with large squares of limestone, a cistern with waterpipes, and a monumental entrance. All alterations and additions made at this time were designed to fit into the Punic scheme and emphasized the portico that surrounded the courtyard. The installations during the Roman Republic period are recognizable by the mosaic floor of small bits of ceramic and white marble which appears in different places over a wide area.[19]

During the I century A.D. the religious life of this sanctuary became gradually less and eventually disappeared entirely at the beginning of the II century. There was no violent destruction but only a slow process of abandonment.[19]

RAS IL-WARDIJA

According to the Italian excavators who worked on it in 1964 and 1965, the Ras il-Wardija sanctuary was, as indicated by the sherds found there, a Punic-Roman sanctuary from the end of the III century B.C. to the end of the I century A.D. It is laid out on a number of terraces, 80 yards to the west of a knoll, on which are the remains of a fallen down tower of unknown date, but probably later than Roman. At the end of the field extending out to the west of the knoll, is an escarp with a large, rectangular recess in it, which has been cut out of the live rock. It is said to be singular and unique in the Punic world. Large niches have been cut into the walls, one of which has the sign of Tanit cut into it (figure 15). On the north wall several crosses and what may be a representation of the god Baal Hammon have been etched. In the centre of the floor at the entrance to the recessed chamber and extending into it is a large rectangular table for offerings.

[19] "Missione Archeologica a Malta", Vols. 1963, 4, 5, 6, 7, 8, 1970.

15. Sign of Tanit

It has a recessed opening on two sides, apparently to allow worshippers to sit on the floor with their feet before them, and it extends to either side at the front of the chamber. On the south side is also a recess with a small bank with two holes for libations.

Running out from the length of the escarp, a wide terrace has been cut into the live rock. On the south side is a large, deep tank or bath with ten steps leading to its floor which served apparently to allow worshippers to enter and perform ablution rights. Near the centre of the terrace is a bell-shaped cistern capped with a rectangular frame formed by cutting away the stone floor of the terrace

72

around it. A long stone bench, cut out of the live rock, runs across the full length of the terrace, apparently to accommodate those watching a performance below. Running in back of it is a corridor, recessed in the rock, and behind that is a stone bank, apparently to allow room for a second row of onlookers. Below this terrace, there are several narrow ones sloping down to a wide, flat terrace covering the whole semicircle at the edge of the cliff which rises some 300' above the sea. During the excavations, the walls of a large building were discovered, which were some 40' in length and had been originally covered with plaster.[20]

It is not known to what deity this sanctuary was dedicated but the sign of Tanit suggests it might have been she (figure 15). In view of the peculiar layout of this complex, resembling an amphitheatre, which may have had a protective wall around the edge of the terrace bordering the point, it was suggested by the Italian excavators that it might have been Baal Margod, the "Lord of Dancing", and that the bench and the terrace above were used to seat those watching the dancing. This sanctuary, which was Punic with many Hellenistic characteristics, is said by the excavators to show the transition from the influence of Carthage to that of Hellenistic Rome.

GHAJN RIHANA VALLEY

On a terrace in Rihana Valley, below Gebel Ghawzara on Bidnija Ridge, is what appears to be an amphitheatre of large, ancient olive trees, which are said to be 2,000 years old or more. They are located within the farm land of the Buhagiar family and one of its members, who lives just to the east of Bidnija Church, will be glad to direct visitors to them.

In all, there are 23 of these magnificent trees. Two are beside the path leading to the main group of 21 that forms the amphitheatre. They are laid out basically in the form of a capital D on an EW/NS axis of two lanes between double rows of trees. The EW lane is some 80' and the NS lane, which is an extension of the entrance path, is about 75' from the basis of the axis.

A double row of trees forming the outer curve of the D and joining the ends of the two lanes, forms within the enclosed area an ellipse about 75' long and 35' at its widest point. It has a level floor which is carpeted with low grass.

Some of the 23 ancient olive trees measure 15' or more in girth. Their trunks, which are rather stumpy, are only some 10', except for one old monster, that has fallen down but still living, has a trunk of about 20'. They have huge limbs four or five feet long, and thin branches which are crowned with a thick dome of leaves, reaching 25 to 30 feet in height.

[20] "Missione Archeologica a Malta", Vols. 1963, 4, 5, 6, 8, 1970.

73

16. Ancient Olive Trees

These trees still bear a black olive which has a thin, soft skin covering a jelly like substance and a thin seed. The trunks and limbs are weathered and gnarled and split in some places, making a bold impression, and those with one side twisting up while the other stands firmly erect, make a graceful composition (figure 16).

Although the old oaks standing in a lap of the hill rising above St. Paul's Bay may not be 1,000 years old, as claimed, it might be possible that these olive trees growing undisturbed in a quiet vale, have actually been growing for 2,000 years or more, especially if the old, fallen monster is an example. It is not un-reasonable to suppose, therefore, that the ancient olive trees still standing may have been planted in neo-Punic-Roman times (300 B.C.–200 A.D.), most probably by the native community that had a rather large settlement on the hill, as their tombs and sherds, which are strewn like pebbles, indicate.

It takes little imagination to believe that this amphitheatre of ancient olive trees was once a sanctuary for holding Punic religious rites and, in view of the elliptical shape of the large, level floor below a higher terrace to the rear, that in the cool of the evening, the members of the community gathered to watch the maidens dancing in honour of Baal Margod, the Lord of Dancing.

CHAPTER VI

TOMBS AND ARTIFACTS

The surface of most of Malta and a large part of Gozo is covered with a strata of Upper Coralline Limestone of up to 530 feet in thickness although often only a few feet. It is soft enough, when not exposed to the elements, to be worked with tools of flint, obsidian and the local chert, on which both the Neolithics and Copper Age man were dependent; and once cut, it retains its shape almost indefinitely. It served ideally therefore for the construction of rock-cut tombs by ancient peoples, with exception of the Bronze Age who cremated their dead, as well as for the construction of megalithic temples, sanctuaries, defence walls, dolmens, and other structures down through the ages and up to the present.

Below the Upper Limestone is a layer of green sand up to 50 feet thick, which is followed by a strata of blue clay that may be up to 230 feet in depth, but often is exposed in large knolls on the surface. It has been utilized for pottery making from the beginning; although it does not compare favourably with some clay deposits in Sicily and Italy, it accounts for the abundant, if not unusually beautiful, artifacts of pottery in all shapes and kinds that remain from the different ages and which represent vividly the development of man during each.

As it was the custom of the various, ancient peoples on Malta to furnish the rock-cut tombs of their dead with pottery bowls, urns, jugs, saucers, vials, etc., to be used by them on their journey to and in the hereafter, the tombs and the artifacts found in them have afforded a fund of information about the activities, characteristics and general way of life of ancient man on Malta, including those of the Copper Age, the Phoenician, Carthaginian, neo-Punic natives, and even the earliest Christians who converted pagan tombs into their catacombs.

TOMBS

The tombs of the Neolithics, if they ever existed, have unfortunately never been discovered. The first known tombs were those of the Zebbug phase about 4000 B.C. They were distributed over an area of about 50 square yards, a mile to the west of Zebbug at Ta' Trapna. They were only about 2' deep but averaged about 6' in diameter. They were paved with flat, roughly chipped slabs made of local stone, and contained a mixture of human and animals bones in complete disorder.[1]

The tombs on Xemxija Ridge above St. Paul's Bay (446878) and possibly the double one at In-Nahhalija, just north of the Golden Sands Hotel (415774), are the only known tombs from the Mgarr phase. Those above Xemxija were used largely in the Ggantija phase and to a lesser extent in the Saflieni and Tarxien phases. There are six of them on the east slope of the apex of the ridge above Pwales beach at the end of the bay. Two of these rock-cut tombs are joined below by a tunnel; the rest are single. They are basically kidney shaped with the outside entrance placed between the two lobes except the double tomb has an entrance above each of the tombs. The maximum breadth of the chambers is from $10\frac{1}{3}$ to $18\frac{2}{3}$ feet and they average 5 feet in height. The entrances of these tombs are placed partially to the side and in most cases consist of a circular pit about $3\frac{1}{3}$ feet in diameter but that of one is about 5 feet in diameter and has two steps leading down into the pit. On the side of the pit is an opening into the top of the tomb through which one can place his feet onto a shelf half way down before sliding onto the floor of the tomb.[2]

The double tomb at In-Nahhalija is just to the east of a farmhouse at the edge of the Naval Rifle Range. This location, according to local legend, was also once a city (belt). These tombs apparently have never been recorded before and are not necessarily what they appear to be, namely, of the Copper Age. The entrance to the tomb, which seems to duplicate the one with steps at Xemxija Ridge is down a path around one Roman cistern and off to the left from a second cistern. It has three steps 15" wide and together 45" long, below which one can step onto the base of the pit and then down onto the floor of the outer lobe of this tomb, which is 7' 4" in diameter. On the side of this lobe to the right of the entrance is a tunnel about two feet above the floor which leads into the second tomb; it is 6' 4" long, 5' 2" high and varies in width from 2' 8" at the base to 2' at the top. Opposite the entrance is a recess in the wall 21" deep and 3' 4" wide, which may have been the beginning of another tunnel. In the centre of this lobe, which reaches a maximum height of 5' 8", is an oval recess in the floor a few inches deep, 3' 2" long and 2' 5" wide. To the left of the outside entrance is an entrance 3' 2" wide at the base and 21" at the top, and almost 4' in height; it leads through a wall 21" thick into the second lobe of this tomb. This lobe is 6' in diameter and 5' high at the centre. On either side of the wall within the entrance of this lobe are semicircular niches some 6" above the floor's edge. One is 3' 6"

---

[1] Evans, 1971, p. 166.
[2] Evans, 1971, p. 112, plans 24, 25.

wide and 2' deep while the other is 2' 7" wide and 16" deep. Both extend upward about 3' to where they come even with the surface of the wall. The floor of the lobe is 5' in diameter and saucer like in shape. At its centre is a rectangular drain 6" deep, 1' wide and 2' 3" long, in which several sherds were found, that may have been from the Copper Age. From the form of this lobe, it would appear that bodies had been placed sitting up in the niches on either side of the entrance. Opposite the entrance are two niches, one 17" × 6" and 6" deep and the other 2' 3" × 5" and 4" deep.

The larger area to which the tunnel leads, appears to have been a cave-tomb, similar to that at Pergla in Xaghra, Gozo, which belonged to the Ggantija and Tarxien phases.[3] Although this cave-tomb has an entrance into it on the east, which may have been cut much later in order to use the area as a shed for animals, it may have originally been entered only by a shaft in the ceiling on the opposite side of the area. The shaft has an oval opening below but appears to be rectangular above and is about 3' × 2' and 3' long. The height of this cave-tomb at that point is 6' 6". This large area is divided partially by a 3' rubble wall extending out from the wall opposite the entrance; the radius of the semicircle on the right side of the centre wall is 8' 8", and that to its left is 13' 8", both of which are 14' alongside the wall. The floor is level, but on the left side of the centre wall is an oval opening in the floor which is 10" deep, 3' 11" long and 2' 8" wide.

There are two types of Phoenician-Punic tombs. The older (VII–II century B.C.) has a more or less square shaft and is found in clusters of up to a dozen throughout the island of Malta. The other, which is neo-Punic, has a rectangular, deep shaft; it was used from the latter half of the II century B.C. until the middle of the I century A.D., and is found particularly near the former Roman city of Melita, especially to the south of its former boundary ditch. On Gozo, there appear to be but few Phoenician-Punic tombs of either type.

At Mtarfa, the hill just to the north of former Roman Melita (Rabat–Mdina) seven tombs (five square shaft and two rectangular, deep shaft) were excavated or cleaned in 1974; they are located just to the right of the road north of the hospital and the keys to the closed shafts of two of them are at the National Museum in Valletta.

The square shaft, older tombs have steps leading down in several of them. To the side of the shaft just above the floor is the entrance of the tomb (in one shaft there had been two). Originally, they were closed with a large block of stone, but these are now missing. One of these five tombs is small but the others are all of the standard type, having a trench at the entrance, a more or less rectangular tomb (the older are curved at the rear) with a low bank at one end

---

[3] Evans, 1971, p. 186.

with head rests for two bodies. At the side of the trench is a bowl cut into the live rock to hold a vase, and on the wall of two tombs is a niche $7\frac{1}{2} \times 6\frac{1}{2}$ inches and $2\frac{1}{2}$ inches deep which was used for a small lamp. The range of measurements for these shafts and tombs are:

shafts: width 4' to 4' 9", length 4' 6" to 5' 2" and depth 4' 6" to 6' 10".
entrances to tombs: width 1' 10" to 2' 11", height 2' 6" to 3' 6".
trenches: width 1' 3" to 2' 1", length 4' 11" to 6' 3", depth 1' 4" to 3'.
tombs: width 2' 4" to 5' 11", length 4' 11" to 6' 3", height 2' 4" to 4' 2".

Of the two tombs with rectangular, deep shafts, one is typical. The shaft, which is only 2' 4" across the top and 3' 1" at the bottom, is 8' 4" long at the top and 7' 1" on the floor, and 13' 2" deep. That it was decided at some time in the II century B.C. to make these tombs more secure by cutting them deeper and such that the mourners could hold their funeral rites less observed, may have been due to some uncertainty with respect to the Roman rulers whose customs were different from those of the neo-Punics. The floor of the shaft had a slight sprinkling of ashes on it, which suggests that the funeral rites were most probably observed there. To make it easier to descend the shaft, it was the custom to cut toe holes into the sides. At one end of the shaft is a large niche shaped in such a way that a mourner could have sat there, although it might have been the beginning of an entrance into a tomb.

The tomb is located through an entrance at the other end of the shaft. A large slab of stone about 5'.high, 3' wide and 8" thick stood before the entrance before it was lowered to the floor. The entrance to the tomb is 4' high, 2' 3" wide and is in a wall 7" thick. The tomb is almost 2' below the base of the entrance. It is 8' 4" long, which is the same length as the shaft, 6' 6" wide and 6' high. To the rear of the right wall is a small, irregular niche, apparently for a small lamp. The back wall is cut at less than a 90 degree angle on one side, and in it is an opening above the floor extending back some 6' which was caused apparently by moisture seeping into the tomb from the shaft of the other adjoining it. On the wall below the entrance appears to be the remainder of a saw tooth design. Otherwise the wall of the tomb have been left entirely without any decoration. In the floor at the right, rear corner is a considerable deposit of black ash and near it were several small bones, probably of fingers, as was required by law during the Roman Republic.

The shaft of the other rectangular, long tomb, which is next to the one described above, is 6' 10" long, 3' 3" wide at the top but widens $4\frac{1}{2}$" on either side four feet down, and about 2" on one end, and it is 5' 10" deep. This shaft had been cut into a cart-rut, as had those of four of the older type of tombs described above. There was no tomb, the shaft apparently having been used for burials instead.

As a number of iron nails about $2\frac{1}{2}''$ long and with unusual, flat heads were found in the deposits of both neo-Punic shaft/tombs, it appears that wooden coffins had been used.

ARTIFACTS

The National Museum in Valletta has an excellent display of Copper Age artifacts from both their temples and their tombs. In the large room to the right off the entrance hall by the desk, are a number of large show cases against the right wall. The third contains the artifacts found in the Zebbug tombs at ta' Trapna. In addition to the head of globigerina shown in figure 5, there are a number of bowls, pitchers, cups, etc. some of which have been restored. The fifth, sixth and seventh show cases there contain the artifacts found in the tombs at Xemxija, all of which are restored bowls, saucers, pitchers, cups, etc.

There are also in this large room a collection of artifacts found in the various Copper Age megalithic temples, and in the next two rooms off to the left from the large room are the artifacts from the Tarxien Cremation Cemetery, including the figurines shown in figure 12. The third room also contains artifacts found at the Bronze Age village sites of Borg in-Nadur and Bahrija.

To the left of the entrance hall is a large room containing some of the decorated stones from the Tarxien Temples, and beyond at the rear is a room containing Phoenician artifacts. The most significant is one of twin cippi of salino marble (figure 17). The two had apparently been in the sanctuary to Astarte at Tas Silg or possibly one to Melkart near it, and were discovered some hundreds of years ago. Reference to them was first published in 1694. Each of them is $3'\ 2''$ in height in the form of a conical fustum with acantus leaves at the base, standing on a pedestal. The pedestal of each is inscribed in both Phoenician and

17. Phoenician Cippus

Greek. That which is now in the National Museum bears the following in Phoenician, which translated reads: "A vow from Abdosir, and his brother Osirxamar, sons of Osirxamar, son of Abdosir, to my Lord Melkart, Lord of Tyre, that he may hear their words and bless them". The other twin cippus was given by Grand Master Rohan to Louis XVI in 1780. Subsequently, it was given to the

79

Louvre and, due to having both Phoenician and Greek inscribed on it, it was from this cippus that the Phoenician language could be deciphered.

On the left side of this room in a case against the left wall are six pieces of Phoenician pottery which were found in a rock-cut tomb at Nigret (Rabat). One of these is a large bowl, tan in colour, without a neck and with two handles; it measures 14″ in height and 10″ in diameter. A larger bowl, also tan in colour, has a neck of about 4″, two handles and is about 16″ in height and 11″ in diameter. There are two jugs, one with a mushroom lip, a neck 3″ long and measuring overall about 8″ in height and 5″ in diameter. The other jug is about 8″ in height and $5\frac{1}{2}$″ in diameter. There is also a typical Phoenician oil lamp, buff in colour, curved over like the palm of the hand up to the wrist, and measuring $4\frac{1}{2}$″ at its widest point. The last is a saucer, a pinkish tan, with two horizontal handles, and measuring 5″ in diameter and about $1\frac{1}{2}$″ in height, In a case to the left in the same room are a small bowl and a cup, both of which are Greek and date from the VII century B.C. All of the pottery described above belongs to a foreign tradition and was wheel made, which was not known in Malta prior to the arrival of the Phoenicians on the Island.

To the right of the entrance of the Roman Museum at Rabat, is a small collection of Phoenician period pottery in the end section of the glass show case. It is placed on shelves lined with orange coloured paper. On the top shelf are local copies of Phoenician and Greek ware, consisting of a burial urn, two vases, two low bowls and two cups. The next shelf contains three small bowls with a handle. Below is a large burial urn, a trefoil lipped jug, two plates, several low bowls, and a fine Corinthian cup of 650 B.C. There is also a trefoil lipped jug on the shelf below beside which are two low bowls. On the lowest shelf is a 7th century B.C. vase with red painted lines and a typical Phoenician oil lamp. On the floor of the show case are three large burial urns of the 7th century B.C. resembling early urns at Carthage and Motya. There are also several pieces of pottery of an early type on the shelf in the next section of the show case, including a vase, a plate, two small bowls with a handle and a small pitcher.

The only other Phoenician pottery on display in public museums is that in the Cathedral Museum in Mdina. In room IV on the ground floor toward the rear on the right of the entrance is a show case against the left wall. On the upper shelf of part 1, there are the following pieces of Phoenician pottery dating from the VII and VI centuries B.C. (dates and attributions were made by William Culicam of Australia): 1. A cup imitating an East Greek shape (not of Maltese pottery and possibly from Sicily), with handles and about 5″ in diameter; 2. Dipper jug 5″ high with one handle from a tomb in Gnien iz-Zghir; 3. Globular jug, 10″ high and about 5″ in diameter; and 4. A two-beaked lamp.

In a glass top case in the hall of the National Museum is a display of various Phoenician-Punic artifacts dating from the VII–V centuries B.C., except two of the cippi date from the II century B.C., and the I century B.C.–I century A.D.

respectively. A collection of small objects dating from the VII–V century B.C. includes: 1. Two alabastra, gold and silver jewellery, and fragments of gold foil; 2. Silver scarab-rings, Egyptian; 3. Bronze amulet and contained inscribed papyrus, Phoenician in Egyptian style; 4. Alabastron with diagonal painted lines; 5. Jewellery; 6. Egyptian gold amulet and fragments of gold foil. There are three cippi: 1. An inscribed stone measuring $8'' \times 3'' \times 3''$, which was found near St. Dominic's Convent in Rabat, and dating from the VI century B.C., is translated as follows: "Stele of melk (a technical term of sacrificial holocaust of a child to the God Baal Hammon) to Baal set up by Nahun to the Lord Baal Hammon"; 2. A rectangular block of stone, measuring about $5\frac{1}{2}'' \times 4\frac{1}{2}'' \times 2''$, and dating from the II century B.C., is inscribed as follows: "The people of Gwl (Gozo) erected and repaired the three . . . sanctuary of the temple of Sadambaal and the sanctuary of the temple of Astarte and the sanctuary . . . during the time of the magistrate Aaish, son of Yail . . . Shaphat, son of Zybegam, son of Abdeshmun, son of Yail . . . the priest Baalshillek, son of Hanno, son of Abdeshmun . . . Baal, son of Kalom, son of Yazer, (being) inspector of the stone quarry Yail . . . the people of God"; 3. Incised on the side of a split piece of stone about $10'' \times 2''$, which was found in a tomb at Hal Far, and dating from the I century B.C.–I century A.D. is a notice as follows: "These are the tombs of Gmr (p?) sh".

In a rock-cut tomb on Mtarfa ridge, which is of the earlier Phoenician-Punic type, a jug was found dating back to about 650–600 B.C., having been left from a prior burial (figure 18). It is trefoil-lipped with a long neck, biconical in shape with a handle, grey in colour, and measures 11'' in height and 5'' in diameter at its widest point. Sabatino Moscati[4] states this type of jug, which dates from the IX–VIII century B.C., became widespread in the VII century and was still produced as late as the VI or V century in some regions.

The only other artifact which apparently belongs to the Phoenician culture, although dating from 500 B.C., is a terracotta anthropomorphic sarcophagus, which was found in a tomb at Ghar Barba near Rabat in 1797 and is now in the rear room on the left of the entrance hall of the National Museum in Valletta. It suggests the figure of a woman, and is reddish in colour. It measures 5' 2'' in length, 2' at its widest point, and with its lid is 1' 4'' high. It is Egyptian in style, particularly the head, which is quite completely formed. The breasts are indicated and otherwise only the toes.

The funeral pottery found in Punic tombs, of the older, square shaft type, is generally dull and repetitious. It is of a relatively poor material, pale buff or reddish in colour, and without decoration except for a painted band of two and sometimes a design of concentric circles on the underneath surface of saucers. Three pieces, dating from about 200 B.C., were found in a trench of an older, square shaft

[4] Moscati, 1968, pp. 80–81.

18. Phoenician/Punic Pottery

type of tomb (figure 18) at Mtarfa. There are numerous examples of Punic pottery dating from the VI century B.C. to the I century A.D. in the National Museum in Valletta, the Roman Museum in Rabat and the Cathedral Museum in Mdina.

Most interesting are four Punic masques, of which three are of women, that are on display in a cabinet at the left end of the entrance hall of the Roman Museum: 1. A head 6″ high with holes on both sides and at the top for placing a string to hold it; 2. A head similar to the first; 3. A head on a long neck; and 4. The upper part of the face down to the upper lip measuring only 4″ high, which may be that of a man.

The National Museum display of neo-Punic bowls, jugs, urns, saucers, lamps and vials in the room to the left of the entrance hall in the rear corner on the right, which had been taken from the rectangular, deep shaft tombs at Tac-Caghki, south-east of the ditch, and elsewhere on Malta, evidences a considerable improvement in quality during the first few hundred years of Roman rule. The saucers especially are of a harder material and clearer red, and an advancement in form took place in shaping some like a small tray, flat on the bottom with straight sides.

CHAPTER VII

COUNTRY ESTATES

The fact that wheat is grown on so many small, marginal plots in Malta today, most of which are still cultivated by a simple, wooden plough drawn by a donkey and harvesting is often carried out by pulling out the stalks by hand, may be the heritage of a Roman order; like other Roman colonies, Malta, no doubt, was required to supply what it could to Italy as it was no longer able to produce enough for itself following the devastations of the war with Hannibal. The production of olive oil, unlike Roman Africa, where the olive trees had to be removed in order to produce more grain and to prevent competition with the production of olive oil in Italy, was not affected in Malta. Much of the food produced in Malta, however, certainly went for the statutory annona or tribute to the Romans.

In theory, it appears, as in Roman Africa, the land belonged to the senatus populusque Romanus, but many of the small neo-Punic farmers, who had been "fixed" on the land by the Carthaginians, were left in possession of their small properties after Roman occupation. As time passed, however, these small properties tended, as they do today, to be divided between the heirs until they were so small that they could not support them. They were then forced to sell out to their richer neo-Punic neighbours, and the former owners were thereby reduced to the status of serfs. The large country estates, which were composed of numerous small plots, and owned mostly by absentee landlords, thus came into existence in Malta in the early part of the Roman period.

The Church, which came to own a number of the large estates, followed an agrarian system similar to other large owners. According to a letter from Pope Gregory (540–604) to Peter, the Subdeacon in Syracuse, under which Malta had been placed, the Patrimony was divided into estates (massae) and let to farmers (conductores) who dealt directly with the peasants (coloni, rustici) and paid the Church official either in money or in kind. The farmers were not to be arbitrarily disturbed in their holdings, and on their death, members of their families were to succeed them. Guardians were appointed if their heirs were still

19. Roman Cistern

under age. The peasants worked a plot of land (fundus) or a part of an estate, and enjoyed the fruits of their labour. They paid only the customary dues to the lord, consisting of the "burdatio", a kind of land tax and a tithe of all the produce which was paid in kind. The peasants were attached to their respective estates, so that they were not allowed to migrate from their lord's estate to another, and they were also bound to contract marriage within this limit and to pay a fee not exceeding one solidus to the farmer. [1]

As it was also the custom to reward Roman army veterans with plots of land upon retirement, some of the large country estates, such as that at Ta' Kaccatura, which had formerly been Punic but later possessed a typical, large Roman cistern (figure 19), and a peristyle in the centre of the house, apparently came to be owned by a Roman. [2]

[1] S. Gregorii EPP. I. 1. (ex: "History of the Church of Malta" Vol. I, 1967, Mgr. Arthur Bonnici), p. 39.
[2] Raven, 1969, pp. 62–69.

Originally, there were probably at least two dozen country estates. The ruins of only a few remain while others, such as those that were apparently located at Rihana Valley, Zammitello, and above the redoubt at Pwales Beach, could be identified only by a disc or the base of an olive pipper found there.

Among the large country estates whose houses are represented by recognisable ruins, are the following which are described below: San Pawl Milqi where St. Paul is believed to have been received by Publius; Ta' Kaccatura; Zejtun; Ghajn Tuffieha; In-Nahhalija; Ras il-Raheb; and Ramla Bay in Gozo.

SAN PAWL MILQI (649769)

The site of the house is a hundred yards above the village of Burmarrad. The large, low plain adjoining the area was at the time of the original occupation, a shallow but navigable bay.

The area of the house, which according to legend, is where St. Paul met Publius, the Roman magistrate, was about 38 feet wide, including a courtyard facing NW/SE, and a bit longer with the end extending under the church. In addition, there were various rooms attached at a right angle which still contain an olive pipper and the ruins of a flour mill.

The first occupants of the site were about 4000 B.C. as shown by several tombs. The site was not occupied thereafter until the Punic period, namely, late in the III century B.C. The earliest parts of the house dated from the end of the II century B.C. The most ancient phases of the house were made up of a type with corridors on the perimeter which resembled closely the African Punic rather than the Roman. Fortifications which dominated the bay, were higher up.

The family, which at first occupied the house, apparently had Punic characteristics, as indicated by utensils and some writing and incisions. In fact, the family's manner of living and acting seems always to have been influenced by African habits. This conforms with other evidence that among the natives, Punic traditions, customs, etc., prevailed until the II century A.D. Also, the elements of the agricultural equipment were Punic.

The existing establishment became a part of the first country house, which was intended not only for agricultural purposes but also for refined living quarters. It is evident that between the Punic installation and the house, there was a continuity and it appears the new installation be onged to the old proprietors.

A fire, which broke out the beginning of the I century, severely damaged the house, causing the proprietors to make a quasi-total rebuilding, and it seems to have ended a particularly flourishing period of life there. In the following phase, from the middle of the I century to the beginning of the II, the eastern zone was abandoned and the industrial installations were concentrated farther west.

There were subsequently different phases of restoration and the house was again made up of refined living quarters as shown by fragments of the painted walls.

The presence of Christians is indicated by a IV century cross in a tile in the floor, a tile with a fish, two stones, one with a cross and the other a fish, and two tridents.

The life of the house continued until the Arab invasion in 870 when they destroyed it. However, they subsequently settled in the ruins, probably because of its cistern.[3]

TA' KACCATURA (574659)

The ruins of this large country house can be reached by a narrow road that goes off the main road some hundred yards north of the Ghar Dalam Museum. It goes down into the ravine and then half way up the hill is a path on the left. After circling around a fallen down farm house, the path continues straight on to the ruins.

Some 40 feet above the ruins of the house is a large cistern cut into the live rock and surrounded by a modern wall. The depth of the cistern is 12' 10" to 13' 9" and its sides are 33' 8" × 33' 6". It is roofed with slabs of rock supported by beams and there are 12 huge pillars each made of stone blocks measuring 2' 8" × 2' 5". The effect upon reaching the floor is like entering a cathedral. To the side of the cistern is an addition which is 3' 3" deeper and its walls are 9' × 8' 6". This type of cistern is not unusual for Roman times (figure 19).

In front of the cistern toward Wied Dalam is what appears to be a jumble of stone blocks but starting down at its original entrance at the lower corner on the opposite side, it is not too difficult to make out the plan. It is a wide entrance and part of the foundation of the porch in front of it can be seen. The entrance comes into the lower end of a corridor leading up the whole length of the house. A few feet up to the right of the corridor is a peristyle, around which the main rooms of the house had been grouped.

The peristyle had 12 columns around a cement floor covering a roof of large stones over a cistern cut into the rock and measuring 12' × 11' 9" and 5' 4" to 6' 6" deep. When overflowing, it fed a bell shaped cistern adjoining it by the corridor and a further one with a rectangular opening.

Going on past the low walls of a room with a floor of live rock on the northwest we come to a block on the ground measuring 4' 10½" by 2' 6" and 1' 11" thick which formed the base of an olive press. It has T shape holes in it which held stone uprights. Though some 2,000 years, it is perfectly preserved, due to

[3] "Missione Archeologica a Malta", Vols. 1963, 4, 5, 6, 7, 8, 1970.

the fact that it had been continuously saturated with olive oil. Another large stone with two shallow depressions is beside it, and a rock cut channel is on three sides.

To the west of the peristyle where the rock floor has been cut to make it level, was a staircase to the upper part of the house above it. On the side of the wall on the left are seven housings cut into the stone for holding the end of the steps. There was also a flight of steps in the corridor a bit higher and just beyond was a doorway to the right leading to the rooms above the peristyle.

Above the house on the west and before the cistern are a number of large and small tanks and vats, cut deep or shallow into the live rock, which were used in the processing of olives. Among them, on the southwest, is a tile covered base which held a large, stone disc for grinding the olives and, running down to the east, was an earthenware pipe, the lower part of which is still in place.[4]

ZEJTUN

When coming into Zejtun on the road leading off the Marsaxlokk road, St. Angelo Church is on the right at the first crossroad. Directly opposite the Church is Luqa Briffa Street which leads to the Government School at the southeast corner of the village. The ruins of an important I–II century country house, which are being excavated at present, are located in a rise of the ground to the rear of the school. The whole unimproved area behind the school is some 250 feet deep and over 350 feet wide. It is bounded at the rear on the south by a stone wall, and on the west is a high wire fence dividing the area from a football field.

The excavated or partly excavated area occupied by the ruins of the country house and an olive oil processing plant adjoining it on the north is about 50 feet from the fence and midway between the school and the wall at the rear. A few feet in front of the wall and about 60 feet from the wire fence are some large, rectangular stones strewn on the ground and farther on to the east, about 50′ in front of the wall, is a well now covered with large stones which belonged to the house.

At the present stage of excavation, the area covered by the house appears to run about 75 feet in a north/south direction and about 80 feet from west to east, and to consist of three main parts: a fairly large rectangular area on the west next to which are three smaller rectangular areas to the east in the centre; farther to the east are two rows of small, rectangular trenches; and at the south corner on the west is an open space on two sides of which are small, rectangular

[4] Thomas H. Ashby, "Roman Malta", 1915.

trenches. On the north are the ruins of an olive oil processing plant running across the width of the area still under excavation and extending out from it by about 45 feet.

The fairly large rectangular area on the west, where there is only a trace of surrounding walls, is $13\frac{1}{2}'$ wide and 34' long, and is covered with a pattern of diamond shaped tiles of brick, the sides of which are $2\frac{1}{4}''$. To the east of this area are three smaller areas similarly covered with patterns of diamond shaped tiles. The one to the north measures $13\frac{1}{2}'$ by $14\frac{1}{2}'$, and the two below it measure 12' by 6' and 12' by 12' and all three are surrounded by dirt walls filled with bits of pottery and measure about 20'' wide and 20'' high. In the centre of the floor of the area on the southeast is a tooled stone, which is round at one end and measures 18'' wide, 20'' long and 16'' high, but for what it was used is not known.

The first row of rectangular trenches farther to the east contains eight and the second row five. They are all surrounded by dirt walls of about 20'' wide and the same in height and measure inside about 10' by 5'.

The space below the larger area with a floor of diamond shaped tiles on the west contains a large rectangular stone $4' \times 2\frac{1}{2}' \times 1\frac{1}{2}'$. A small trench within dirt walls is on the south and on the east are two such trenches. The one next to the tiled areas above has a channel in its floor that may have been a drain or a conduit for water.

The area covered by the olive oil processing plant is divided into three parts. The first part adjoining the larger tiled area contains a circular basin which was used as a settling tank; it is cut into a stone and measures 4' in diameter and 2' deep. A few feet to the northeast is a large stone, like that at Ta' Kaccatura, which served as the base for an oil press. It is 6' 3'' long, 2' 8'' wide and 2' high. It has T shaped holes on either end to hold the uprights of the press and a round hole in the centre. On one side is a concave recess and on the other is a small hole where the oil flowed out into a channel below that led out some feet at first above ground and then below. There is also a channel to the left which runs to a deep hole in the live rock.

The second part of the olive oil processing area is composed of four rectangular areas to the east. The one in the centre has a large, rectangular stone with a square hole in it which presumably held some appliance. The rectangular area below has a large, rectangular dressed stone recessed in its floor that appears to have been taken from a temple or some other fine structure.

The third area farther to the east contains a semicircular channel which apparently was used to bring waste water to a large cistern which is now covered with boards. To the north beyond the cistern is a large, rectangular stone in a wall, across the end of which is another wall of large stones, and beyond that is still another area strewn with large, rectangular blocks of stone.

GHAJN TUFFIEHA

This country house and bath, now known as the Roman Baths, is located in a valley, just to the left of the road from Zebbieh, a short distance before reaching Il-Fawwara (422762). The area covered originally by the house and the thermae or bath was about 160 feet square, the lower or southern half being for the house and the upper half, adjoining the cliff on the north, being for the bath. There are only a few walls of typically large Roman stone blocks remaining where the house stood, but the lower portions of the walls of several rooms and fixtures which formed the facilities for the bath have been restored wholly or partially.

The house with the thermal bath was formerly considered to have belonged to a high Roman official, possibly the same one who owned the palace (villa) at Rabat. However, in view of the country estates that belonged to some of the richer native members, it seems more likely that this was occupied by such a family, at least as long as the house and agricultural complex existed. It is estimated that the house was built at the end of the first century or at the beginning of the second. The base of an olive pipper still on the field above affords evidence of a function of the estate.

The key to the gate of the compound is kept at a farmhouse at the end of the paved road. A young man there will act as guide if desired.

The path leading north and straight ahead from the gate passes in front of a small building on the right enclosing a mosaic floor with a geometric design within which are groups of four small umbrella like shapes.

A few feet along the path, also on the right, is another larger building enclosing a rather large, square mosaic floor containing a beautiful design radiating from a circular marble plaque, like the rays of the sun; it is presumed to have contained a fountain in the centre, which provided warm water to the occupants of this tepidariam or heated chamber. Two large, stone blocks of the original wall and one on the floor to the left remain, but the broken benches in front of them were possibly installed when the room was restored.

A few feet on, the path turns left into a corridor paved with diamond shaped brick tiles. On the left are the remaining, lower portions of thick walls of typically Roman blocks of stone, measuring 3' by 20'', which formed a large room, rectangular in shape, except for the southwestern side where it curved. It was the furnace room for heating the water in containers above it; these appear, from the remains of the arched pillars, to have been at the height of the tepidarium into which the hot water flowed. Tile lined conduits surrounded the furnace room. A mortar lined, open cistern 4' 11'' by 2' 7'' and 3' deep is on the northern side of the furnace room near the end of the corridor.

On the right side of the corridor are the walls of a privy; it had several toilets remaining intact when excavated in 1929–35. Apparently, there were three on either side and at the back. This might indicate that they were not for the family that lived originally in the house but that the bath was extended after the house ceased to exist and may have been for use by a nearby garrison. It appears, however, that this privy was exactly the same as old Roman privies in general, and was, therefore, for household use. The benches containing the toilets were replaced after excavation of the room but they are the same as the originals which had long, horizontal slabs along their front side that could be removed for cleaning. In front of the benches is the original shallow channel around the sides and back of the room, which was paved with diamond shaped tiles. The large stone block at the entrance of the room contains a round recess at its centre, which was the socket for holding the pivot of a revolving door to ensure the privacy of its occupants.

Next to the privy, are some low walls of a room which also had a floor paved with diamond shaped tiles. Inside the wall is a small, rectangular open cistern, which was to be filled through pipes leading from the outside; the guide may tell you it was for babies!

Out in the field to the south is a rectangular area, rimmed by the remaining, lower part of three walls and containing a floor with diamond shaped tiles. To the east of it is another group of such tiles which are not surrounded by a wall.

To the east of the path from the entrance gate and extending out between the tepidarium and the room toward the entrance, is a long 80′ corridor; its floor is covered with diamond shaped tiles, varying in size from 4″ to $5\frac{1}{2}″$. A stone water conduit with rectangular pipes formerly ran along its northern edge toward the reservoirs on the west.

Immediately to the left of the corridor, and behind the tepidarium, is a tank 9′ 10″ square and 4′ 7″ deep; it has cement lined walls and a floor originally covered with mosaics of red and blue squares. Three steps lead down into it from the side of the tepidarium; it was no doubt used for the customary cold dip following the heated bath.

On the right side of the corridor, there was originally a row of five rooms presumed to have been for changing clothes. They all appear to have had connecting doors, and floors that had been covered with mosaics throughout. Shelters were built some years ago over the remaining portions of the mosaics.

To the right of these rooms and bordering the path leading from the entrance gate, a large space has been excavated; it is assumed it was once a swimming pool fed from the spring above. This spring, now enclosed in a small building with an iron door, supplies about 80,000 gallons of water daily to the main water lines of Malta.[5]

[5] Bulletin of the Museum, Vol. (1929–35).

IN-NAHHALIJA

On an isolated plateau, close by a hill to the west, is a farmhouse that until some years ago was occupied (408777). This L shaped building 100' long and 35' across stands on a site where a country house was located in the Roman period, and, as evidenced by the tombs described in Chapter VI, had probably been used since early in the Copper Age.

There is considerable evidence that a country house stood on this site in Roman times. Large size, rectangular blocks of stone, measuring about 30" long, 20" wide and 18" thick, which seem to be typical of those made by the Romans, are found in the walls of the farmhouse, the rubble walls around it, and within the tombs alongside; even the walls of the girnas on the side of the valley to the north seem to have a few in them, while some walls along the road in the nearby village of Manikata contain an unusually large number of such big blocks of stone. By the side of the outside staircase at the end of the farmhouse is a shallow bowl cut into a stone block 17" × 16" and beyond, on a pile of stones, is a rectangular stone 2' × 10" and 3" thick which has a circular hole in it that could also be from Roman times. There is also a quantity of Roman period sherds and broken bits of Roman type bricks, both heavy and thin, scattered around in back, and some plaster made of cement and fine bits of pottery can be found there as well.

Most important, however, are the two Roman type bell shaped cisterns. One is located at the end of the L shaped courtyard of the farmhouse. Its opening in the live stone is 5' long and 2' 2" wide, but some 5' below it is oval in shape, extends out to a radius of about 10' and is 10' to 15' deep. The other cistern, which is similar, is located at the end of a path to the east beside a wall, at a corner of a field.

Next to the cistern in the courtyard is a half of what was once a very large bowl, beautifully made of coralline limestone; it is some 5' in diameter and 14" deep with a flat centre below the rim which is 6" or more in thickness. This bowl was probably used for processing olives, which would indicate that the cultivated fields surrounding the house on the east and the south once were covered with olive trees. Beyond, to the south, according to local legend, there was, like Tas Silg and Wardija in Gozo, a "city" (belt) in former times.

To the north of the house, within an area surrounded by a rubble wall, is a rectangular area cut into the live rock. It measures about 9' by 4' 6". When filled with water from the winter rain it could have served as a reservoir but, although it is now roughly shaped at the top, it might be the rock filled shaft of a Punic tomb. The evidence points more, however, to a Roman occupant than a neo-Punic farmer. Possibly, the owner-farmer was some soldier veteran who had been rewarded by his Roman governor.

RAS IR-RAHEB

On the north end of a promontory, beside a sheer cliff above the Bay of the Wind (Fomm ir-Rih), was what appears to have been a country house (395740). It was located on a terrace surrounded on three sides by a low wall forming a loop. That portion of the wall, which is located in front a few feet back from the cliff, and extends from east to west for over 200', is constructed of large blocks of stone. The house was centred in the enclosed area behind.

The stone foundation walls of the house, which are recessed in the ground, extend over 50' from east to west across the back and are about 86' from south to north. These foundation walls are of large, rectangular blocks of varying sizes; one large one toward the front is 9' long and 2' wide. A number are wider than the rest of the foundation, and in some places the foundation appears not to have been of stone blocks but of the live rock. In the foundation on the west near the front of the house, a large rectangle had been cut into the stone measuring 3' 2" long.

The foundations of two walls appear to have run across the inside of the house. One is about 11' in from the rear wall, and the second is about 45' beyond toward the front. As there are no wall foundations within this enclosed area, it is presumed that it contained an open court. On the southeast end of this area about 6' from the east foundation wall of the house is a large, flat stone 2' 3" × 2' 8", which has the letters UY cut into it. A few feet to the west are two flat stones measuring together 4' × 5'.

Some 5' 2" in front of the cross wall foundation on the north is an area bordered on the inside with walls, which is located at the northeast corner of the house; it measures 25' from south to north and 18' from east to west, and has an uneven floor of cement. The foundation wall on the south is of two rows of stones; in the outer row is the remainder of what appears to have been a brick conduit for water, and inside the second row is a pattern of a few diamond shaped brick tiles and stones which covers a small part of the floor. Near the northeast corner of the room is a round hole, recessed in a double square frame of stone, which no doubt was a drain, indicating that the room was the bath of the house. The north/south foundation wall of this room extends for another 30' to the north beyond the east/west wall of the house. The terrace wall of large, stone blocks is located another 30' beyond.

Alongside the rear wall foundation of the house near its east corner, are two large megaliths, some 8' high and each is about the same in length. As the promontory is directly below the Bronze Age village site located on the ridge of Il Qlejgha, it is possible they had formed a part of a defence wall, similar to those described in Chapter IV, in back of which it appears the inhabitants would have placed themselves in case of attack, with only a short space between them and the cliff above the bay.

Extending out from the megalith on the east, is a foundation wall running 12' to the south where another wall runs 10' to the east, to a line even with the east foundation wall of the house. There is a large, broken stone on the floor measuring 3' 8" × 2' 2". A few feet to the west in the open area to the south of the megaliths is a large, rectangular stone partly buried, with two square holes cut into it. It may have been the base of an oil press, such as is found at other country houses; if so, it is the only indication found that the fields covering this large, flat promontory had once been covered with olive trees.

Some 12' to the east of the southeast corner of the house is the frame of a cistern made of a single block of stone measuring 4' 4" × 3' 4" and containing a hole about a foot in diameter on one end. Below it is a rectangular opening about 2' × 5', which extends downward for about 4' before widening out into a bell shaped recess about 10' across and the same in depth.

Directly to the north about 10' from the cistern is a row of large stones running 45' by the side of the house, and from its end on the south, another row of stones runs out for about 20' to the east. A similar row of stones extends out to the west from the south wall of the house for about 30'.

A quantity of sherds and pieces of pottery, which could be restored, were brought up from the bottom of the cistern a few years ago, along with some pieces of bronze, iron, glass, etc. They are now on display in the Roman Museum at Rabat. The pottery, which was mainly of the Imperial period, showed a mixture of Punic and Roman influences and suggested a date between the I century B.C. and the I century A.D. for the building. From this evidence, and the rather crude nature of part of the stone foundation, on the one hand, and the precisely cut stones, on the other, such as that over the cistern, it would appear that the people who had lived in the house had been neo-Punic natives who had profited from the more advanced architectural forms introduced by the Romans. That it was a country estate, is suggested by the large cultivated areas on the promontory but, in view of the difficulty in reaching this remote point, it would not seem to have been a useful location for a country retreat. On the other hand, the wide scattering of sherds of the early Roman period over the whole promontory would suggest that a "city", such as at Tas Silg, had been located there, which might indicate, as Dr. Trump has observed, that the building located on the point had served a religious purpose instead.[6]

RAMLA BAY, GOZO

At the end of a lush valley, which possibly formed the estate, and at the edge of Ramla Bay, was a large country house and bath during the Roman period.

[6] Trump, 1972, p. 127.

It was excavated in 1910 but unfortunately had to be covered over again to protect it from vandals and the sea. There is now a large mound of sand there sprinkled with bits of decorated plaster from the walls of the house. Possibly, it will be uncovered some day and a wall built around it to protect it.

The house contained 11 rooms while 7 rooms adjoining it composed the bath. Upon excavating the house, it was found that rather high walls were still standing around most of the rooms of the house. Except for the thick walls still standing around the room that contained the cold bath, only the foundations were left of those belonging to the bath. Five of them had consisted of a hypocaust (hot room), and one, which had a marble floor, had been a waiting room.

On the south toward the sea, the built on area was 66' across, and from the south to the north, where the rooms were fewer and came against a hillside below Calypso's Cave, it was 87'. The building had been constructed of blocks of local stone, measuring up to 5' 3" × 1' 7" and 1' 2½" thick each, most of which showed signs of previous use. The construction was poor, the walls were not coursed while the interstices were filled only with clay. The walls of the room against the hillside were the best preserved and were over 3' deeper on the inside than the outside, and the wall toward the sea was 7' 6" thick at the bottom.

In an angle of the room next below was a low seat where, next to the wall, a telemon was found; it was the upper part of the torso and head of a nude and youthful satyr. In two rooms adjoining the bath, which might have been dressing rooms, benches were also found. The floor in one of them was covered with diamond shaped tiles. The room with the marble floor, which measured 15' 2" square, was apparently the finest in the building.

On the outside wall of the cold bath was a channel to receive the waste water and a further course of 33' led from it toward the sea, which can still be seen beyond the mound of sand.[7]

[7] Thomas Ashby, "Roman Malta", 1915, pp. 70–74.

CHAPTER VIII

ROMAN MELITA, GAULUS, DEFENCE TOWERS, PORTS AND ROADS

Already toward the end of the Roman Republic, life on Malta and Gozo appears to have benefitted from the example of Rome in adopting for itself the arts of Greece and in lavishing its wealth on sumptuous and costly decorations of houses and a profusion of mosaic pavements. Diodorus Siculus, a Sicilian historian, who lived until 21 B.C. or later, appears to have come to Melita about 40 B.C. when he wrote: "To the south of Sicily are three islands each of them with towns and harbours offering shelter to all ships cast thither by storms. The first is Melita, 800 stadia from Syracuse, having many convenient ports. The inhabitants abound in opulence, for they have artifices for every kind of works; but they excel most in their manufacture of linen which is beyond anything of the kind both in firmness of its texture, and its softness. Their houses are very beautiful and magnificently ornamented with pediments projecting forward and the most exquisite stucco work. The inhabitants have become very wealthy and increased in reputation and splendour".

From the evidence afforded by the antiquities of this period, which have been found in and around Melita and Gaulus, the islands appear to have continued to thrive under the atmosphere created by Emperor Augustus (27 B.C.) for a golden age of literature, Roman art and sculpture, spacious nobility, sound engineering and efficient administration. Then, toward the end of the II century A.D., the harmony that had existed between rulers and the ruled in Malta began to diminish as Christianity emerged in strength.

At the beginning of the Imperial period, as evidenced by the inscription previously referred to with respect to the restoration of the temple to Proserpine by Chrestion, a procurator of Malta and Gozo under Augustus, the islands were no longer under a propraetor of Sicily but became governed by a direct representative of the Emperor and/or Senate.

The towns of Melita and Gaulus in Gozo each had in the period of the empire, a full Roman town constitution. And from the evidence afforded by an inscription in Greek, which was interchangeable with Latin during the first three centuries, a citizen of Gaulus was enrolled in the "tribus Quirina" of Rome during the administration of Tiberius (14–37 A.D.), which indicated that the rank of "municipium" had been given to Gaulus. A similar title was given to Publius, who received St. Paul in 60, which may have indicated the same for Melita, but certainly that distinction had been given it by the II century as certified by a contemporary monument.

As the security of the islands from attack became assured under Roman protection, the natives abandoned their less accessible settlements on remote ridges and promontories, and except for those on the country estates, many of which had their own fortifications, it appears the concentration of the population in the walled cities of Melita and Gaulus was completed during the I century A.D. This movement may also explain in part why the sanctuaries at Tas Silg and Ras il-Wardija, together with the "cities" adjoining them, gradually became abandoned during that period.

With the development of the cities of Melita and Gaulus, the neo-Punic population came to adopt Roman manners, usages and modes of social intercourse as well as Latin names, often spelled in Greek, and, with the existence of a high degree of culture and the industry of the native population, a considerable degree of prosperity of trade and agriculture came about. But whether the native population became thoroughly Romanized is doubtful.[1]

MELITA

The Roman city of Melita, which stood on a site that had been occupied possibly by the Phoenicians and certainly by the Carthaginians after them, is on a flat topped ridge, almost in the centre of the island. The ridge runs SSW and NNE; and from its south-eastern corner, it slopes downward gradually to a point, at the base of which is now a moat 1,000 feet across, which was constructed by the Arabs after they occupied the island in 870 A.D. The point appears possibly to have been smaller than it later became during the Arab occupation. It may have ended on a line running west from the northeast corner of the present Cathedral. From the top of a wall of large, coralline limestone blocks, which is standing above a deep, wide cut in the live rock beneath a house on the north side of St. Paul's Square, it appears that a bastion may have extended west to the corner of St. Peter Street and Magazine Street. This possibility is supported also by a similar cut in the live rock under the Cathedral, which is in line with the above, and a long tunnel vault under the Carmelite Priory at the opposite end. The west side of the wall extended to the west rim of the present park above

[1] Thomas Ashby, "Roman Malta", 1915, p. 75.

the Roman Villa where, as shown by the Roman blocks still there, it turned toward the valley to join the end of the ditch at Via Ghar-ixem. The east side of the headland above the cliff, and extending south up to where the road enters Saqqajja Square from below, appears to have remained about the same. The whole area from the bastion on the north to the ditch on the south was about 2,000 feet within a circumference of about 12,000 feet.

The gate to Mdina inside the moat, which is now placed a few feet to the west of where it formerly stood, opens into a square. At its end, a road around the old nunnery of St. Benedict enters into Villegaignon Street, on the left of which is the house of the Inguanez family. It appears from the numerous, large fragments of marble structures, still extant, which were found in the courtyard of the nunnery and discovered in 1747, while digging the foundation of the Inguanez house, that the temple to Apollo and a theatre belonging to it must have been located there during the I and II centuries A.D.

The Cathedral in Mdina, according to tradition, is on the site occupied by the palace of Publius, the governor, where St. Paul came and cured his ailing father.

Outside the moat at the south corner of Melita, a Roman period villa was excavated a few years ago. To the north, according to A. A. Caruana,[2] was the site of a Roman praetorium, which was located just to the west of the estate that may have been that of the Roman representative of the Senate, which is now called the Roman Villa and over which the Museum of Roman Antiquities has been constructed. In the valley below at Gnien is-Sultan (Garden of the Sultan) the ruin of an important Roman building was found in 1909–10, which was made of beautifully carved Malta stone. Beyond the ditch on the south, according to A. A. Caruana's plan of Roman Melita,[2] was the place of assembly for public and commercial transactions, and from there, extending out 2,000 feet and across the whole southwestern boundary of Melita marked by the ditch, was the burial place for Melita from its beginning.

The Ditch

While Gela on the coast of Sicily opposite Malta has its Greek wall with every stone still perfectly bevelled, Rabat still has a large part of its Roman ditch cut into the live rock 2,000 years ago. It ran 2,600 feet across the whole southwestern perimeter of Roman Melita. Until eight years ago, a half of it leading west from the Parish Square had never been covered over, and to the east of St. Paul's Church on the square, most of it still remains as it was. Looking out of the rear window of St. Paul's Church, which was built over the ditch in 1683, a stretch of the ditch can be seen extending out 500 feet. And to the east of Buskett road it runs 400 feet to the cliff on the eastern edge of Rabat.

[2] A. A. Caruana, "Pagan Tombs and Christian Cemeteries:', 1898, p. 85.

The eastern end of the old wall of Melita still remains much as it was beyond where the road comes up to Saqajja Hill. It skirts around the promontory on which the Saura Hospital is located and comes to the east end of the ditch. The whole side of the promontory still shows where the live rock had been cut away to form the wall which was extended upward by blocks of stone by 10' to 15'. A ledge, about 15' to 20' wide, runs all along the front of it.

The east end of the ditch is only some 60' across, as the wall of live rock along the east extends out beyond both its sides to form what appears to have been lookout points. The 400' stretch, which was originally 82' wide and 12' deep is filled with soil which is sprinkled with sherds from the Roman period and apparently former ages. Above the live rock forming the side walls of the ditch the foundations of buildings have been built up to the junction of Saura Street and Buskett Road on which they face. And where the ditch comes to the junction between them, there is a drop of about 25'.

The 500' stretch of open ditch begins again just beyond a row of buildings and is divided twice by cross walls before reaching the rear wall of St. Paul's Church: The two sides are also lined by houses or a wall that runs beside Alley No. 1. Several houses have gardens bordering the ditch which have paths leading down into it. The ditch is still its original 82' wide and its 12' wall of live rock remains on either side, above most of which the foundations of houses have been built. On its south side there are a number of caves, some of which were extended into shelters during the War where animals are now kept, and beyond which were catacombs now blocked off. At one point beside the wall, a well had been cut, possibly in ancient times, which is still used. It is circular in shape with a diameter of about 5'. Its walls are lined with toe holes on either side about every 2' and it is unusually deep, going down about 70' to where it opens into a channel with water flowing through it.

On both sides of St. Paul's Church, there were once caves receding back from the ditch for a number of feet. The most famous is now known as St. Paul's Grotto where, according to tradition, he slept during the three months he was on the island. The present grotto was only a small part of the original cave which extended to at least the wall of St. Paul's Church and now also forms the landing at the bottom of the stairs at the entrance of the grotto and a large crypt of the Church of St. Publius which was built over the site in 1692 to replace a chapel erected over the grotto in 1617.

The cave on the north side of St. Paul's Church is entered by a flight of stairs below a small building a few feet out from the Church. At the foot of the stairs is a small shrine said to have been built in the III century, and the cave, which has been decorated and lighted, extends some distance beyond. Half way up the stairs a plaque is in either side of the wall; one is of St. Peter and the other of St. Paul, both of which are considered to have been placed there in Byzantine times.

A door to the left of the stairs leads into what is said to have been the Roman prison where there are the traditional V shape perforations in the stone but unlike those which are placed on the sides of walls for holding animals, they are in the ceiling!

There were two main gates of Melita with bridges over the ditch; one was located at the junction of Saura Street and Buskett Road on the east, the foundations of which were found 12' below the present level of the road, and the other was at St. Cataldus Street, which then formed apparently the west side of a square where the main streets leading to the punic tombs and catacombs began. A third gate and bridge may have stood at the west end of the ditch where it came to a cliff on the side of Wied Ghar-ixem. A path, presumably Roman, still crosses over to Gnien is Sultan.

The Temple of Apollo

In the Cathedral Museum in Mdina, at the back of Cathedral Square, there are several relics in marble which apparently came from the Temple of Apollo. Two are on the left in the hall by the courtyard at the end of the entrance hall. The more important is an inscription in Latin on a flat piece about 17' square and 3' thick. This inscription, which is dedicated to Claudius Justus, is attributed to the I century A.D.; it was discovered in the nunnery of St. Benedict in 1868 and donated by Dean Vincent Vassallo to the Cathedral. It reads as follows:

CLAUDIUS JUSTUS, TRIUMVIR AND PATRON
OF THE MALTESE MUNICIPIUM, BUILT AND
CONSECRATED AS HE HAD PROMISED, A
MARBLE TEMPLE WITH ITS STATUE AND ALL
ITS PROPER ORNAMENT AND IN EXECUTION
OF THIS WORK SPENT MORE THAN HE
PROMISED.

It is tempting to believe that the Claudius in question was the Emperor who reigned 41 to 54 A.D., which is presumably about the date the temple was built, but from the wording of the inscription, it seems he is considered to have been a native of Malta.

The next most important piece is placed high on the wall above the inscription. It is a most perfect and beautifully carved large rectangle which may have been an entablature of the temple (figure 20). It was discovered in the courtyard of the nunnery of St. Benedict only recently. This nunnery, where no men are allowed to enter except the doctor, the whitewasher to "sterize" the walls and a gardener, was using it as a bench and they were not aware of its carving underneath. However, the gardener happened to notice it and reported the fact to the Curator of the Cathedral Museum. Negotiations commenced and eventually the

20. *Entablature of the Temple of Apollo*

Museum received this most important relic and in return a large bench of marble now stands in its place in the courtyard of the nunnery.

One other marble relic, which the Curator states came from the nunnery of St. Benedict, stands on the floor of the hall to the right side of the entrance; it is a piece of Roman fluted column identified at late I century A.D.

Several more marble fragments of the Apollo Temple may be those found in the Roman Museum in Rabat. Three of them are against the wall opposite the entrance. They are: 1. a large, triangular corner of the ceiling which apparently had been supported by a small column; 2. a right-angled horizontal piece of a cornice, and 3. a rectangular piece of an entablature. The first and third appear to correspond to those shown in a drawing in Abela-Ciantar (tab. XIV) which Caruana[3] states are, together with those shown in (tab. VII), from the Temple of Apollo. This statement appears to be borne out by the following: 1. all of the pieces concerned apparently belong to the Corinthian order of architecture; 2. they all appear to date from the I or latest the II century A.D.; 3. the cornice in the Roman Museum seems to fit over the entablature there; and 4. the similarity of the design of the carving on the frieze of the latter with that of the entablature in the Cathedral Museum would indicate that at least these three pieces, and presumably also the fragment of the ceiling, have the same origin, i.e., the Temple of Apollo. It is to be noted, however, that the type of marble used for the entablature in the Cathedral Museum is not the same as that of the pieces in the Roman Museum, and may therefore have been produced when the Temple was extended as indicated below. The temple also seems to have had a small as well as a large part. This is indicated by the size of the entablature in the Cathedral Museum, which would have been in the small part, and by the two sizes of capitals to be seen at the right end of the Roman Museum behind the olive pipper.

A large marble relic of the Apollo Temple, which was found in digging the foundation of the Inguanez house, is now standing at the head of the stairs in the Roman Museum in Rabat leading to the rooms of the Roman Villa (palace) below. It was apparently the base for a statue (not found), both sides of which are broken off. An inscription in Latin is in the centre which is remarkably

[3] A. A. Caruana, "Report on the Phoenician and Roman Antiquities", p. 89, paragraph 93.

preserved otherwise, considering it is attributed to the II century A.D.[4] The first two or three lines of the inscription, which presumably gave the name of the individual in whose honour it was inscribed, are wanting. Translated, it reads thus:

"the first of all the Maltese of the Municipality erected an altar; he also consecrated the theatre of marble to Apollo; he also erected the four pillars in the vestibule, the parascenium (stage), and the podium (a projecting low basement); in all work he spent 110, 798 sestertii by his own liberality. In acknowledgement thereof the Maltese by a general collection of money erected a Statue"[5]

Roman Period Villa at Saqqajja

In 1965, when part of a garden was being cleared to construct two houses at the corner facing both Main Street and Nicola Saura Street, workmen came across parts of the foundations of a house that had been built during Roman times. Excavation revealed the walls and floors of three rooms running NE/SW. The first room has a mosaic floor consisting of red pottery with white marble tesserae inset at intervals; the same kind of tesserae also formed a diamond shaped pattern enclosed in a border of two lines along the centre of the room. The floor of the second room contained a mosaic consisting of only white marble tesserae. The floors of both rooms were supported on rows of two handled peg-based amphorae placed upside down with their necks inserted into a layer of clay on the bed rock; the object in using these amphorae as a foundation was presumably to keep the rooms dry. The third room had a floor of much finer quality; a thick layer of mortar and stone chippings, pounded to a smooth surface, covered it. There had been conduits for water passing underneath.

The villa dates from about the beginning of the I century A.D. and it appears that the original house continued in use up to the end of the II century, as shown by the presence of sherds of African red slip ware which was imported in considerable quantities at that time. The house fell into disuse early in the III century and remained so until the XV–XVI century—a vivid, although silent, commentary on the history of Malta during those many centuries between the decline of Rome and the coming of the Knights of Malta.[6]

Roman Villa at Rabat

This villa was built on such a grand scale that it might be supposed that it was a palace of the governor or some other high Roman official. The foundations of

[4] Thomas Ashby, "Roman Malta", 1915, p. 30, (attributed to Dr. Hulsen).
[5] A. A. Caruana, "Recent Discoveries at Notabile", 1881, p. 10–11, item no. 8.
[6] Report on the Working of the Museum Department for the Year 1965, p. 3.

about two dozen rooms have been excavated and more may have been cut away when the road down to Mtarfa was constructed. The ground plan of the building could be determined from the foundations of some of the rooms and traces of others. The plan of the main part of the villa is shown on the side wall at the top of the flight of steps leading down to it. The main room at the opposite end of the lower floor contained a large peristyle which was surrounded by a portico with 16 columns, enclosing a compluvium leading to a cistern. To the left of the landing at the bottom of the steps are two rooms; the nearer is indicated on the plan by the letter C, and that beyond by the letter B. In front of the peristyle towards the east, directly below the main entrance to the museum, was a porch with two columns. Adjoining room B but now outside the wall of the building of the museum, was a large room identified by the letter E, which had a mosaic floor of green, black and white marble slabs. Next beyond was room A. There are the foundations of numerous others in the area surrounded by an iron fence.

The centre of the area toward the rear appears to have been an extension of the villa; it has floors of several rooms paved with small bits of red ceramic inlaid with small squares of white marble, such as found at Tas Silg, which dates from the Roman period, i.e., I century B.C. to I century A.D. One of these rooms was apparently enclosed by a portico with columns. The left side of the area appears to have been occupied by a series of farm buildings, including those for farm equipment, such as an olive pipper, the base of which is still standing there.

One large room on the south, partly cut off by the fence, contained a mosaic picture of Autumn. Traces of the exterior wall show also that a wing of the building likewise extended towards Mdina for about 100 feet or more. Cut in half by the excavation of the road down to Mtarfa appears to be the underground remainder of a pendentive (bathing room), which may have been furnished with hot water from the furnace room to be seen behind the clothes washing room half way up the road from the old railway station to the road running below the bastion of Mdina.

The rooms identified by the letters C, and B, which adjoined the peristyle, were probably the most important. There were doorways between the two rooms and with the peristyle, some with one or two steps and closed by doors and others with no doors. Both rooms, as well as the compluvium enclosed in the peristyle, had mosaic pavements. That within the peristyle, which was 22' 4" square, was exceptionally beautiful. In the centre of this mosaic is a rectangular picture of two doves drinking from a bowl; the fact that the doves face away from the porch on the east is believed to indicate that the main entrance of the villa must have been in the area to the west surrounded now by the iron fence. Above the columns of the peristyle on the opposite side from the landing of the steps leading down to this floor, is a fragment of the entablature which formed part of the original structure. Below it is a part of one of the original columns of the portico. On the near corner of the peristyle is the original frame over the cistern.

A rectangular fragment of the ceiling of the peristyle is located at the north-west corner of the ground floor, supported by blocks on either end and with a mirror beneath. The amphorae on the walls surrounding the room containing the peristyle were found under the mosaic of the compluvium in 1921–3 when it was being restored.

In the hallway to the south and in front of rooms C and B, are a number of marble columns which, together with those on either side of the landing below the stairs, are said to have formed the facade of the villa.

On the wall above the shelf to the right of the peristyle are two mosaic pictures found on the floors of the villa when it was excavated. Both of them, though damaged, are most interesting and attractive. One, which was on the floor of room A, is an inlaid marble slab, measuring 2' by 2'1", of highly superior work-manship; it shows a nude male figure whose feet are tied with cord, a lion's skin beneath and a club at his feet. A female figure on the right is engaged in binding his hands. Another female figure on the left has a pair of scissors in her right hand and with her left she is holding the beard of the male who is in evident distress at being deprived of it. The drapery is very elegant and its folds well arranged, with bright colours and various shades. The whole composition is exceedingly well grouped and executed with precision. It is considered most likely to represent an episode in the life of Hercules when he was to be sold by Zeus to the Lydian Queen Omphale, as it was decreed that he should serve as a mortal for three years as an atonement for having killed Iphitus, son of the King of Aechalia. The other mosaic picture, which had been on the floor of the room outside on the south, and measures 1' 10" by 2', is inlaid in hard lime. It is of a young man with curly hair, representing Autumn. In one of his hands he holds a bunch of grapes entwined with parts of the vine, and in the other a pomegranate. A dove is flying toward the grapes and a duck is on the left of the picture.

Three pieces of sculpture, also found in the ruins of the villa, are on the shelf. From left to right, they occupy the following places:

1. The lower part of a leg and a foot in a kind of stocking and on a low pedestal (several remains of colossal statues are in the cabinet on the far wall to the left; they include two hands—one with a signet ring on the third finger—and a foot).

7. A fine portrait bust in close-grained white marble with the tip of the nose broken, 1' 8" high, of the type of Agrippina the younger.

9. A statue of a male figure 4' 6" high wearing a Roman military cloak, said to be a rather good work of Greek art. The figure is without arms and head; there is small cavity where the head and neck could have been fitted.

Three other statues found in the villa stand on the left of room C; from left to right, they are as follows:

1. A headless, erect female figure, 5' high, with long chiton and himation which must have veiled the head. The left hand and forearm are missing.
2. The figure of a boy in a toga, 3' 9" high. It is lacking the head, both arms from the elbow and both feet.
3. The lower half of a draped female figure, 4' 9" in height. The figure is represented as advancing, the right leg is drawn back and off the ground. The drapery is very carefully treated and the knees are visible through it.[7]

Among the other articles found in the ruins of the villa were four brass coins of various emperors, i.e., Gordian, A.D. 238–243; Aurelian, A.D. 270–275; Constantine II A.D. 337; and Constantius II A.D. 337–360. There were also several bodkins of ivory, some inches long, to fasten the hair; some pieces of wind instruments made of bone, showing clearly the finger stops; and a large quantity of fragments of earthenware vessels, etc.

Museum of Roman Antiquities

A number of Roman antiquities, which were presumably found in Malta and Gozo during the past several hundred years, were originally included in the Library Museum until 1903. Thereafter, they were displayed in the old National Museum opposite the Cathedral in St. John's Square until they were transferred to the Museum of Roman Antiquities in Rabat after it was built in 1921–3. Many of these, which were placed in storage in World War II, were never recovered.

In addition to the fragments of architectural structures identified in the section on the Temple of Apollo and those found in the ruins of the Roman Villa described in the previous section, a number of the Roman antiquities from the old collection, which are now on display in the Museum, have been identified from references made to them by A. A. Caruana[8] and Thomas Ashby.[9] These, together with other antiquities displayed there whose identity was already known, are described as follows, according to their location in the first floor of the Museum, beginning at the wall on the left end of the room, proceeding along the rear wall opposite the main entrance, and continuing along the wall on the right end to the show case on the right side of the entrance where three are to be seen above it.

[7] A. A. Caruana, "Recent Discoveries at Notable", pp. 3–10.
[8] A. A. Caruana, "Report on the Phoenician and Roman Antiquities", 1881.
[9] Thomas Ashby, "Roman Malta", 1915.

1. In the centre of the show case against the left wall, are two Roman masques, probably of the I century A.D., such as were used in Greek and Roman times in the theatre to denote comedy. The larger one on the right (figure 21), which had small holes on either side and could have been worn, was found in the 17th century in the Roman ruins when constructing a house on the north side of St. Paul's Square, Mdina. It was a part of the De Piro collection until recently when it was donated to the Museum by Mr. and Mrs. A. A. Cassar Torreggiani.

2. Next to the show case, at the left end of the rear wall, is a large rectangular stone on the

21. Roman Masque

floor, bearing on the left end in front a carving of a comedy masque and a lyre on the right end. Within the framed space is an inscription in Greek, which has been translated as follows: "Dedicated to the Gods of the underworld. Publius Aelus Hermolaus, a comedian and a lyre player from Pergamus, lived 25 years. Farewell". It is believed to date from about 150 A.D.

3. Three funerary bas-reliefs of the II century B.C. are on the shelf above.

4. A marble plaque, said to have been found at Mtarfa and showing two Greek soldiers capturing a Trojan soldier.

5. Marble statue of a woman, without head, etc. which may have been one of a group with no. 6 and no. 9. Provenance unknown although it might have come from the Temple of Proserpine on Mtarfa.

6. Statue representing a Roman Goddess (possibly Proserpine) (museum no. 26) found at Mdina. It is 6' high, including the base; the forearms and head are missing; two birds face inward across the breasts; and the figure wears pointed shoes. The drapery indicates it is a work of the Roman period, but the hair falling over the breasts, shoulders and back, and the numerous necklaces with which the figure is decorated show a Phoenician/Punic influence. The statue is said to have stood in the 17th century at the gate of Mdina.

7. Three marble bas-reliefs of Roman work, high on the wall, represent Tentisilea (museum no. 47) on the left, Zenobia (museum no. 49) on the right, and Tuliola M. Tullii F. and Claudia Metelli (museum no. 48) in the centre. They are said by M. Bres., Book V, chapter VI, to have been recovered from the

105

remains of a temple on the shore near St. Angelo in the XVI century. They were apparently kept thereafter in the Grand Master's Palace until possibly the 19th century.

8. According to Abela, book II, not. VI, paragraph V, the stone bearing an inscription (apparently later broken and restored) was discovered at Mtarfa in 1613. It records that Chrestion, freedman of Augustus and Procurator of Melita and Gaulus, repaired the pillars, the roofing, and the walls of the Temple of Prosperine, which were ready to tumble down on account of their antiquity, and that he also gilded the hall. When the inscription was found, it appears it was more or less intact; only the words in small type, which were supplied by M. Bres and others, were missing:

CHREstion. auG. L. PROC
INSVLarum. MELIT. ET. GAVL.
COLVMNAS. CVM. FASTIDIIS
ET. PARIETIBVS. TEMPLI. DEAE
PROSERPINAE. VETustate
RVINAM ImminEN
tibus . . . . . . res
TITVIT. SIMVL. PILAM
INAVRAVIT

A. A. Caruana, who investigated the place of origin of this temple on Mtarfa, where there is now a statue of a Saint, found nothing, but stated that a marble portion of the temple of Proserpine, bearing an inscription in Greek (a prayer of adulation to the diety), was over the main entrance to the Auberge of Italy. It is now in the courtyard of the main Post Office.

9. Statue of a woman (museum no. 64). Provenance unknown but may have been one of a group with nos. 6 and 5.

10. Small figure of a female (museum no. 63) said to represent Venus coming down to the sea.

11. Statuette of Artemis (museum no. 50), Greek (Parian?) marble, 10" high. The goddess is moving to her left; the quiver at the back is fastened by a strap above the shoulder; both breasts are bare; in the right leg had been an iron rod; at the back, by the left leg appears to have been a dog which also may have had an iron rod in it. Provenance unknown.

12. Circular "oscillum" (formerly museum no. 52) 11" in diameter, bearing on one side a female dramatic mask with high-piled hair and open mouth, and on the other side a griffin rampant, with a ram's head beneath its left claw. Found in Gozo.

13. Greek vases, late Attic, V to IV century B.C., found in Rabat about 1825. Identification cards are below each.

14. Etruscan cinerary caskets, VIII to VII century B.C. Said to have been brought by a private collector and donated to the Museum.

15. Male head (museum no. 58), $13\frac{1}{2}''$ high, damaged, style similar to that of Damophon; Pentelic marble with white crystals. Provenance unknown.

16. Male portrait-head (museum no. 62), 9'' high, 222–235 A.D. Hair hammered, eyebrows also hammered; pupils rendered by incised circles; head much polished. Probably found in Malta.

17. Male bearded head, apparently blind, (museum no. 59); wearing a cowl; alabaster. Provenance unknown.

18. Male figure 4' high (formerly museum no. 29); draped with a toga; found in 1747 (?) near the nunnery of St. Benedict (possibly connected with the Temple of Apollo).

19. Male torso, youthful, 24'' high (museum no. 61); right arm was raised, left hanging by side; short locks to nape of neck; back worked; there is a large "puntello" on the right hip, a small one on the left hip, and two more a little above the left knee. Provenance unknown.

20. Head of Antonius Pius, Emperor 138–161 A.D. (museum no. 57); $17\frac{1}{2}''$ high, pupils rendered by bean shaped segments; beard and moustache shown by thick clustering locks. Provenance unknown.

21. Cornice slab (below the shelf at the right end of the room) found at Gnien-is-Sultan (described in following section). Two other pieces are on the ground floor, against the west wall, below the left end of the shelf containing Arab tombstones.

24. Olive pipper, standing on the floor; said to have been found at Marsa-xlokk.

25. Portrait-bust of youth, 8'' high (museum no. 51); fat, sleepy and rather Etruscan looking; Pentilic marble (?). Provenance unknown.

26. Female portrait-bust, 8'' high (museum no. 54). Flat features, featureless smile on face, bony structure, kerchief over head with ends crossing in front; hair parted and waved back. Provenance unknown.

27. Male portrait-bust (museum no. 55) 7'' high; short hair and whiskers, flat features, a little Phoenician in character; Pentilic marble (?). Provenance unknown.

28. Head, almost bald of old man with grump expression (museum no. 67) now on ground floor at left end of shelf to the right of the peristyle); 10'' high; nose almost gone; perhaps of the republic period. Provenance unknown.

Roman Building at Gnien-is-Sultan

Gnien-is-Sultan (Garden of the Sultan), apparently was given its name in Arab times, but as indicated by the antiquities to be found in the area, it was already an important suburb of Melita in Roman times. Roman field walls appear in a number of places. Rich farms with fine Roman cisterns, subsequently restored by the Grand Masters of the Knights of Malta, are still to be found there. And in the fields within high rubble walls dividing the different parts of this lush area, chunks of marble and marble tesserae, diamond shaped tiles, sherds of a cup etc., pieces of alabaster ornaments, bits of black lava from Mt. Etna that had been formed into mortars, and angles of concrete are to be found there; all are of Roman origin as are the large blocks of coralline stone taken long ago by a farmer from some Roman wall or building to build a rubble wall.

In the district of Ix-Xaghra, within Gnien-is-Sultan, there is little to show now that a beautiful building of local stone had been built there by the Romans about the II century A.D. The most notable landmark there is a former Norman style chapel with its unique interior arches still intact, but in a field just to the west, there is on the side a pile of large blocks of coralline limestone, such as the Romans quarried, and in the centre of the field is a stone standing that had been dressed apparently to form a part of a building which may have been that from which came the three structural fragments now in the Roman Museum in Rabat.

The latter were discovered in 1909 when a field was being prepared for planting a vineyard, and the workmen came upon sherds of Roman pottery and fragments of glass and marble in the soil. The director of the Museum undertook the excavation of the area which continued into 1910.

Fragments of marble slabs of different colours were obtained in abundance, together with sherds of fine pottery, tiles, bits of mosaic and carved globigerina limestone. The foundations of walls were found on the bed rock; the remains of a large cistern, one side of which was concrete, were also discovered.

However, the most important discovery was the three slabs of Malta stone, which had formed part of the horizontal cornice or drip of a Roman building. They are exquisitely worked and, though damaged, the director of the museum stated that no stone ornamented so delicately had ever been found in these Islands. The building, which must have been fairly small, was considered to have been erected in the best period of the Roman occupation. Its destruction was complete, however, and the fragments from it had been widely scattered during the long period between the time it fell into ruin and the cultivated terraces there were formed many centuries later.[10]

ROMAN GAULUS

As with the location of Melita, the Roman capital of Gozo (Gaulus), the sister island, which likewise bore its name, occupied a site on a high plateau in the centre of the island. In addition to the citadel, which rises over some 100

[10] Reports on the Working of Government Departments, 1909–10. p. E7.

feet from the plateau at its northern extremity, the town probably spread out during Roman times over much the same area as that now occupied by Rabat (Victoria). And again like Melita, the Arabs reduced its boundaries after 870; it was limited in form and extent to that of the Castello, by which name it came to be called, which was further reduced to its present walled area after it was besieged in 1551 by Barbary pirates and practically the whole population of 6,000 was taken in slavery to Tripoli.

Although trial excavations within the Castello have revealed nothing earlier than medieval, evidence was found in 1960, when a sewer trench was cut across the main square of Rabat, that an accumulation of debris, extending some 12' below the modern pavement, contained evidence of occupation from the Middle Bronze Age to the Punic, which was followed by the Roman when several buildings had stood there. As had happened to the area outside the walls of Mdina, the area around the Castello seems not to have been kept up after the decline of Roman occupation until that by the Knights.

Within the old Castello still surrounded by walls towering above the surrounding plains, a large part on the northeast has been left apparently as it was following its devastation in 1551. Wandering among the low, fallen walls and in the open fields there, one cannot escape the feeling that, in addition to the "Norman" ruins, one is surrounded by much that was Roman. Peering deep into the openings of the drainage system, large blocks can be seen framing the channel, such as might have been placed there originally by the Romans. At the corner of a field bordered on the northeast by ramparts, is a large rectangular stone with a deep incision on either end and one in the centre that probably once held a Roman olive press. Behind the Museum are Sally ports in the wall and a Roman inscription on a large block, broken off at the bottom, is in the north side of the old gateway.

According to tradition, the cathedral of Gozo, which occupies the centre of the Castello, is on the site of a temple to Juno. The remains of Doric columns and blocks of marble were discovered in rebuilding the cathedral, and were lying in the streets in the last part of the 18th century. A. A. Caruana[11] produced a picture showing a headless statue without arms of Julia, wife of Augustus Rex, which stood in a niche in the outer wall of the Castello probably from the I century, when the

22. *Statue of Julia Augusta*

[11] A. A. Caruana, "Report on the Phoenician and Roman Antiquities" 1882, p. 136–7.

worship of the emperor and the imperial house prevailed in the islands; it is now to be seen in the Museum to the right of the entrance within the walls of the Castello (figure 22).

This Museum, which is housed within the beautifully restored Casa Bondi, has an excellent collection of antiquities ranging from the Neolithic down through the Copper and Bronze Ages, and the periods of occupation by the Phoenicians, Punics, Romans, Arabs, Normans and other European dynasties and the Knights of Malta. They are well identified and exhibited. The statue of Julia is on the first floor to the right at the top of the steps. In the room on the right of it are a number of Roman anchors and jars recovered from the seabed, but the main display of Roman antiquities is in the first room on the ground floor to the left of the entrance. From left to right, they include the following:

1. A part of a base of an olive pipper of coralline limestone found at Xewkija, Gozo.
2. Head of a satyr in a niche within the left wall.
3. Three inscriptions in Latin against the rear wall as follows:

a)   CERERI. IVLIAE. AVGVSTAE
DIVI. AVGUSTI. MATRI
TI. CAESARIS. AVGVSTI
LVTATIA. C. F. SACERDOS. AVGUStal
IMP. PERPETVI . . . AVG
M. LIVI. M.F.QVIe. oPTATI. FLammis
IVLIAE. AVGVST. IMP. PERPET
LIBERIS . . . SIbi . . . CONSACRAVit

This inscription dates from the time of Emperor Tiberius (14–37 A.D.); it was dedicated by Lutatia, daughter of Caius and a priestess of Augustus, and by M Livius, son of Marcus and a Flamen Augusti, to Livia Drusella, wife of Tiberius Nero. After Livia divorced her husband, she married Octavius Augustus, who admitted her as a member of the Julian tribe. Hence her name became Julia Augusta. During her life time, the Romans worshipped her as one of their goddesses, giving her the names of Ceres, Juno, Venus and Diana. The inscription has no known provenance.

b) C. VALLio. QVIR. POSTVmo MUNICIPPI. pat
imp LADRIANI. PERPETVI. IIIIV. QVINQ. DCVR. IV. DI.
inter. QVATRINGENARIOS. A. DIVO ANTO
nino Pio. OMNIBVS. HONORIBVS. CIVITATIS. SVAE. HO.
norifE. FVNCTO. ITEM. LEGATIONE. GRATVITA APVD
imp. HADRIANVM. ET. APVD. AMPLISSIMVM. ORDINEM
DE. novaLIB. REDHIBENDIS. PLEBS. GAVLITANA. EX
AERE. CONLATO. obPLVRA. MERITA. EIVS. D.D.

110

This inscription came to light in 1736 during the construction of the Capuchin Church and convent. It records that the people of Gaulus subscribed towards its erection to honour C. Vallius, patron of the Municipium and one of the four Magistratia of the order of Decurions of Hadrian, elected every five years. Antonius Pius (138–161 A.D.) had also made him one of the four hundred Decurions, as he had served honourably in all capacities in his own town as a legate in the court of Emperor Hadrian and as a member of the order for the restitution of ships.

c) CESTIO. L. F. POAMPI. GALLO. VA
RENIANO LVTATIO. NATALI. AEMI
LIANO. PATRONO. MUNCIPII
L. MARCIVS. MARCIANVS. AMICO OPTIMO
V. KARISSIMO. SIBI. HONORVS CAVSA. S. L.

Marcus Marcianus set up this inscription to honour his best and dearest friend. Cestius Lucius, son of Poampus, patron of the Gozo municipium. It was found in Gozo in 1622.

4. On the shelf by the right wall are the following:

a) A foot of a Roman statue found within the Castello.

b) A small replica of a leg in bronze.

c) A sculptured head of a youth.

d) A small statue of the legendary wolf suckling Romulus and Remus. It was found in Rabat, Gozo, in 1720.

e) A neo-Punic inscription of the II century B.C., which is described in Chapter VI under the artifacts in the National Museum in Valletta where there is a copy of it.

5. A photograph, on the wall to the right of the entrance, is of the inscription on the side of the old entrance gate, mentioned above. It reads as follows:

M. VALLIO. CF. QVIR. RVFO EQVO. pu.
BLICO. EXORNATO. A. DIVO. ANTONI
NO. AVG. PIO. PLEBS. GAVLITANA. EX
AERE. CONLATO. s.p. OB. MERITA. ET. IN.
SOLACIVM. C. VALLI. POSTVMI. PATRO
NI MUNCIPPI PATRIS ENS
. . . . . . mATE . . . . . .

The people of Gaulus, wishing to honour Marcus Vallius, son of C. Vallius, patron of the Municipium, who had been knighted by Antonius Pius for his merits, subscribed towards the erection of a statue and this inscription, thereby pleasing also C. Vallius, the father.

DEFENCE TOWERS

The beginning of difficulty for Roman domination of the Mediterranean appears to be evidenced by the round towers built at strategic locations in Malta probably about 269 in association with the incursion of the Heruli from the Black sea. Apparently an attack was anticipated on the south of the island where the ruins of three of the four round towers still to be found are located, i.e., ta' Gawhar at Tal Bakkari (544644); ta' Wilga, west of Mqabba, (situated in a field $\frac{2}{10}$ of a mile at 512676 up from where the road bordering it comes to the southwest corner of the Luqa Airport enclosure; and ta' Hlantun near Gudja (552674). The fourth round tower, of which little remains, is ta' Cieda near L'Imsierah (531740).

The most impressive of these towers is that of ta' Gawhar at Tal Bakkari. It is surrounded by a large, flat area divided by numerous walls within which are rather strange, uncultivated fields covered with a carpet of low grass. In the centre of each is a large pile of large pieces of coralline limestone which have been split rather than quarried in blocks, and which presumably had been placed in such a way that they would impede those bent on attacking the tower.

The tower is placed on a mound and must have extended upward some 30' to 40' at least. It is 40' in diameter. Underneath it is a large cistern about 20' square and about as deep, which is similar in size and construction to that at ta' Kaccatura (figure 19). The outside wall on the north and northeast still reaches up about 25' above the mound. It is made mostly of tremendous rectangular blocks of coralline limestone measuring up to 5' in length, 4' in width and 3' thick. At the southeast corner is an entrance to the inside of the tower where there is a rectangular room of about 10' by 15'. Two of the soft globigerina limestone blocks making up the interior wall on the west have been scooped out, possibly to form shallow shelves. That could have been done by the occupants of the farmhouse that had been placed beside the tower, but more likely this was done by bored Roman soldiers who only waited for an attack that never came.

PORTS AND ROADS

The principal interest of the Romans in Malta was no doubt its strategic location as an entrepot at the crossroads of the main route between the east and west Mediterranean, and between Italy and Sicily and the Roman possessions in North Africa. The port, generally used by them appears to have been that at Marsa Creek, which formerly extended up into the low area beyond for some distance. Roman masonry has been found along Stables Street on the north side of the Marsa sports ground, where apparently quays and warehouses had been during that period.

Below Corradino Hill, the foundations of two extensive groups of warehouses were discovered in 1766–8, each consisting of 15 or more rectangular store rooms, and measuring about 115′ × 80′ and 100′ × 65′ respectively. On both sides of the larger building was a cistern cut into the rock, the smaller measuring 50′ × 20′ and the larger 50′ square. In one store room 260 amphorae, the usual containers for not only wine but also other produce, were found. The coins found ranged from III century B.C., when Rome occupied Malta, to 829 A.D., a few years before the Arab occupation. A quay wall of large stones was found on the south side and roads seem to have led from it and other points on the shore to the store houses.

From the collection of coins in the Museum, bearing dates during the II and I centuries B.C. up into the I century A.D., it appears that the trade with Malta was mainly by ships from the eastern shore of Sicily; many of the coins were from Messina, indicating that, as in prehistoric times, Malta was still a pivotal point for ships sailing between the east Mediterranean and the west through the strait of Messina.

One of the roads leading into the interior of Malta from Marsa appears to have been that seen at the junction of Wied Kbir and Wied Qirda where it rises to the ridge that leads directly into Siggiewi. It is bordered on either side by flat, rectangular blocks of stone, fitted closely one to the other, and with cobble stones in the centre.

Another harbour which was used in Roman times was at Burmarrad, below San Pawl Milqi, to where the bay reached at that time. Beyond, at Salina, was also a Roman port as shown by the lead stocks and collars of Roman anchors found on the sea bed there. Likewise, St. Paul's Bay was an important harbour; the stock of a Roman anchor weighing 3 tons was brought up a few years ago at Bugibba. Above Pwales Beach, at the base of the Bay, is what appears to have been a Roman road bordered with flat, rectangular blocks of stone with cobble-stones between. It leads up and around a rectangular building of large blocks of stone, which may have been placed there as a kind of pillbox, although it was once used for beehives. Mellieha Bay was also used by Roman ships as confirmed by the investigations carried out there in 1967 of a wreck during which a number of artifacts were discovered, including glass vessels, large and small domestic pottery, wide-neck amphorae, and mortaria of the I century A.D., etc.[12]

In Gozo, Marsalforn Bay is, according to tradition, where the Romans had their main port for that island. Xlendi Bay was also used on occasions as evidenced by the wrecks found there of two ships; one was sunk in about the II century B.C.; the other in about the V century A.D., and Roman jars and anchors recovered from it are now on display in the Gozo Museum.

[12] Honor Frost, "The Mortar Wreck in Mellieha Bay", London, 1969.

113

CHAPTER IX

CATACOMBS, SHRINES AND BASILICAS

The development toward, if not the emergence of Christianity among the native population of Malta, appears to have commenced in various places on the Islands of Malta during the latter part of the I century and continued gradually into the II century when, in the latter part of that century, the Church of Malta took control and organized the worship of those who welcomed its tenets, with the result that Christianity appears to have become generally recognized as the religion of the Maltese natives already by 200. Thereafter, it appears to have become widespread throughout the Islands, despite persecution by the Romans which, although apparently not exercised seriously before about 250, appears to have been particularly severe thereafter until 306 when it came to an end. In 313, after Constantine became Emperor, Christianity was tolerated and peace was restored definitely in 330.

Following the decrees of 381–5 by Theodosius I, which nullified pagan rites of ownership to their religious sites, the Church established chapels beside some of the catacombs that had been developed under its direction, and took possession of both the shrine of St. Paul at San Pawl Milqi and the former neo-Punic/Roman sanctuary at Tas Silg where it established a basilica.

Either sometime during or just at the end of the IV century, following the division of the Roman Empire, it appears Malta was placed directly or indirectly under the administration of Constantinople. During the V century, Malta disappeared from history, due probably to its occupation, first by the Vandals and later by the Ostrogoths who succeeded the Romans in Italy. In about 535, when Malta appears to have been conquered by the Byzantines, it came under the jurisdiction of the Eastern Empire. The Church of Malta, however, seems to have remained under the Pope until about 756, when it was placed under the Byzantine Church of Constantinople, only to disappear after the occupation of Malta by the Arabs in 870.

CATACOMBS

The catacombs of Malta are the key to understanding the development of religious beliefs and the emergence and spread of Christianity in the first centuries. The principal evidence found in them with respect to their dates of origin are the sherds of pottery remaining from bowls, vases, amphorae, etc., that had been placed in them by the families of the deceased when they were inhumed there. Collections of sherds obtained from a number of catacombs have been analyzed by Professor Pasquale Testini and his assistant at the Institute of Christian Archaeology, University of Rome, and by Mr. Tancred C. Gouder, Archeological Curator at the National Museum of Malta, the results of which are given in the table on p. 116.

The hundred odd sherds that have been analyzed are not, of course, a complete collection of the various types of pottery originally placed in the catacombs, and consequently they represent only some of the periods during which the catacombs in question were in use. They appear to confirm, however, a continuity in the development of catacombs generally from the I century through the IV and that many of the catacombs continued in use up into the VIII century or later.

That the remaining sherds and sometimes restorable pieces of pottery found in the tombs had been placed in them at the time of inhumation and were not brought from elsewhere after the tombs had been discovered and opened, is believed to be established first by the prevalence with which the sherds appeared in the order of the periods to which the respective types of tombs seem to have originated. And second, by the fact that if they were mixed with others, it was invariably only with those of the succeeding periods of early Christianity.

That the custom of placing types of pottery in the tombs, other than the ampules for perfume, which are self explanatory, was maintained by the early Christians and the Jews, possibly in the belief that they should be available to the deceased in after life, seems, moreover, not to have been affected by the basic difference in their religious beliefs as opposed to those of the pagans from whom they inherited the custom.

Origins

As stated in chapter VI on Tombs and Artifacts, the deep shaft type of tomb introduced about 150 B.C. following Roman occupation of Malta, might indicate that already at that time the neo-Punic native population considered it necessary to make their tombs for the dead more secure. About a century later they expanded their shaft/tombs by not only placing a tomb at either end of the floor of the shaft but also divided each tomb by a trench so as to accommodate a body on each side. Soon thereafter, as indicated by the gradual abandonment of the

DATES OF SHERDS FOUND IN THE CATACOMBS BY CENTURIES

CATACOMBS	VII, VIII	V, VI, VII	V, VI	V	IV to VI	IV, V	IV	III, IV	III	Late II, III + IV	II to IV	II, III, IV	Late II to III	II, III	Late II	Early II	I to V	I to III	I, II	I A.D.	I B.C.
Cave under Mosta Fort			+	+				+						+					+	+	+
L'Abbatija tad Dejr					+									+				+	+	+	+
Bingemma	+		+	+		+		+	+	+	+	+		+	+		+		+		
Salina									+			+									
Ghar Gerduf																		+			
Secondary School for Boys at Rabat															+	+					
Catacomb No. 23	+									+				+		+					
St. Agatha's Church (old)									+												
St. Catald Church			+			+		+					+								
St. Agatha's Church (newer)									+												
St. Agatha's Church Jewish									+												
Catacomb No. 12						+				+											
Catacomb No. 10																			+		
Catacomb No. 13			+			+															
Catacomb No. 14						+	+														
Catacomb No. 17A								+													
Catacomb No. 22						+															
Catacomb by No. 14		+												+							

sanctuaries during the I century A.D., large numbers of the native population appear to have rebelled against the enforced religious beliefs of the Romans, which included a strong patriotic element and the deity of the Emperor. As a result, some of them sought out various remote places where they could bury their dead without fear of being disturbed. Some of these were in caves on the side of hills and soon they began to build a number of tombs into them. Others were cut into the side of hills, and passageways with tombs on either side were developed that eventually became large catacombs.

At about the same time, some of the families living in Melita took to extending the shaft/tombs of their forefathers, which abounded outside the ditch forming the border of the capital on the south and made them into catacombs, each with a few tombs. Toward the end of the I century or the beginning of the II, the funeral clubs, whose members may have been among the last to abandon the sanctuaries, built a number of catacombs in the area adjoining the Melita ditch. These catacombs, which are unique among those still existing, were exceptionally well laid out and excavated. As described in the section on The Agape, moreover, they were especially equipped to perform a funeral rite, including a libation for the dead, which proved to be a forerunner of the agape introduced by the Church in the second half of the II century.

The development of the funeral clubs in Malta as well as in Rome came about as a consequence of the restrictions imposed on the right of meeting and of private association as from 64 B.C., when a number of colleges suspected of plotting against the Government were suspended by Julius Caesar. These restrictions were continued by Augustus, Claudius and Trajan. However, an exception was made in favour of the funeral clubs, which were first established possibly before the I century and became very numerous in the II and III in Malta as well as in Rome, particularly during the reign of Septimus Severus (193–211).

Burial corporations of several trades were recorded in Rome under titles such as Collegium Faenariorum. Corpus Fabrum, Navalium, etc. In Malta, such corporations were also formed; as the incisions in the stone slab in catacomb no. 3, and in the wall of no. 23 indicate, one was an association of the physicians and surgeons and the other of fossors (who constructed the catacombs). In Rome, some funeral clubs bore the title of special worshippers, such as Cultores, Jovis, Apolliuus, Herculis, Dianae, etc. Also, some burial clubs, with a limited number of members, belonged to private foundations, and Roman soldiers had their own, which were maintained by regular contributions from their pay. The privilege of association for the same purpose was likewise extended to the poorer classes by law.

An inscription pertaining to one of the burial clubs was discovered in 1862 in the ruins of Civata Lavina, twenty miles from Rome. This corporation was constituted in 133 by a permit from the Senate to provide a decent burial place; its members styled themselves worshippers of Diana and Antonius (110–130), a favourite of Emperor Hadrian who honoured his memory by having him deified.[1]

De Rossi, the great authority on the Roman catacombs, observed and pointed out the bearing of the numerous and varied burial clubs upon the development and use of their catacombs by the early Christians.[2]

In Malta, it appears from the evidence found in the catacombs of the funeral clubs, that it is possible to go much further in interpreting the role that they played. It appears, in fact, that their members, who were among the better educated or skilled craftsmen, were the principal link in the transition from Punic beliefs to those of Christianity. At the time of St. Paul's shipwreck on Malta (60 A.D.) they were, no doubt, already well advanced in their search for a more meaningful religion, and by the middle of the II century they had become proto-Christians if not actually Christians. It remained apparently only for the Church of Malta to organize the form of their worship. This is evidenced by the transformation of their catacombs, and especially the mode of celebrating the agape in conformance with the precepts of the Church. The English version of the Catholic Encyclopaedia[3] states in regard to the "reformed" funeral clubs the following:

"The faithful united in bodies, guilds, corporations or colleges. These seemed to have differed but little from those of the pagans, in respect, at all events, of the obligation imposed by the rules of incorporation. . . The establishment of such colleges gave the Christians an opportunity of meeting in much the same way as the pagans did - subject always - to the many obstacles which the law imposed. Their feasts. . . and the Supper with which their meetings ended might very well have been allowed by the authorities as a funereal one. In reality, however, for all faithful worthy of the name, it was a liturgical assembly".

The Jewish catacombs appear to have originated with three multiple tombs, dating from the I–II century. Some years later they appear to have been developed into catacombs, and at the end of the III or the beginning of the IV century the form of their catacombs underwent a distinct change due to the installation of the agape tables which indicate that some or most of them had been converted to Christianity.

With the transformation of the form of the catacombs belonging to the funeral clubs, some of them as well as a few belonging to various families were acquired by the Church of Malta during the II–III century and subsequently

[1] A. A. Caruana, "Pagan Tombs and Christian Cemeteries", 1898, p. 26.
[2] A. A. Caruana, "Pagan Tombs and Christian Cemeteries", 1898, p. 26.
[3] The Catholic Encyclopaedia, 1907, Caxton Publishing Co., New York.

were developed into large complexes, such as those of St. Paul's Catacombs and the older one at St. Agatha's Church.

The Agape

The English language version of the Catholic Encyclopaedia[4] states the following in reference to the agape: "The celebration of funeral feasts in honour of the dead dates back almost to the beginnings of the worship of the departed, that is, to the very earliest times. The dead in the region beyond the tomb, were thought to derive both pleasure and advantage from these offerings. The same convinction explains the existence of funeral furniture for the use of the dead. Arms, vessels, and clothing, as things not subject to decay, did not need to be renewed, but food did; hence the feasts at stated seasons. But the body of the departed gained no relief from offerings made to his shade unless these were accompanied by the obligatory rites. Yet the funeral feast was not merely a commemoration; it was a true communion, and the food brought by the guests was really meant for the use of the departed. The milk and wine were poured out on the earth around the tomb, while the solid food was passed in to the corpse through a hole in the tomb."

In Malta, there is no evidence that the celebration of the funeral rite for the dead included food, although it may be presumed that it did. But evidence can still be found of the practice of the libation rite, beginning with the Copper Age people in their temples, the Early Bronze Age, as evidenced by the recession in the top of some of their dolmens, the Phoenician-Carthaginian in their sanctuaries, and continued with the neo-Punics in their catacombs. The catacombs of the neo-Punic funeral clubs all contain various installations in them for this purpose. The best and most complete example is that under the Secondary School for Boys at Rabat.

This catacomb, which has been identified by the sherds as being in use in the first half of the II century, has two rectangular rooms, behind the walls of which are chambers containing groups of tombs. The rooms have a number of stone benches in them for seating the guests and, most indicative, there are large slabs of stone extended by wide, rectangular plugs at the back to fit into the stone frames of the chambers and seal off the tombs. In the top surface of these slabs, sometimes within a diamond shaped design, is a hole the size of the index finger which extends through the slab and comes out in back just above the plug. That these apertures in the stone slabs were used for performing the rite of libation is evidenced by a prayer, written in neo-Punic, and divided into five parts, each of which appears above the entrance to one of five chambers

[4] The Catholic Encyclopaedia, 1907, Caxton Publishing Co., New York, N.Y.

recessed in the walls of the second rectangular room. This prayer, each part of which is given below as a line, follows:

On the strength òf the gift offered to you
Here the duty of piety
Oh, you who are powerful
Be assured, abstain (from harming us)
This is the propitiatory sacrifice.[5]

This extraordinary libation rite, made in honour of the deceased, and not apparently to a deity, was obviously symbolic, as the corpse within the tomb could not have been touched by the liquid poured through the aperture in the stone when it had been placed into the frame of the tomb chamber. But certainly it was believed that its cooling effect would not only cause the spirit of the deceased to refrain from harming the one who made the libation but also bring some good upon the giver by interposing with the deity.

The purpose and form of celebrating the agape feast in the catacombs of the Christian world appear to have been changed rather suddenly by the Church. The Italian language version of the Catholic Encyclopaedia[6] states: "The agape appeared in some churches as an organized institution in the second half of the II century, and assumed the meaning of a communal repast." This transformation from the celebration of funeral feasts in honour of the dead to one of a communal repast, held under the auspices of a priest, seems to be indicated by the composition of the replacement of the original catacomb under the Secondary School for Boys in Rabat by one which, according to the sherds, was used during the second half of the II century.

The original catacomb described above is to the left of a flight of steps; the replacement is on the same level but to the right of those steps. The entrance into the latter is located beyond a passageway between the two catacombs. Within is a rectangular room with four bare walls and an entirely flat floor. In the centre of this room is a rectangular, dressed block of stone some 2' × 3' and about 16" high. It has a raised rim around it except in the centre of the long side on the left. This stone block, which appears definitely to have been a hastily constructed agape table, might reflect a sudden decision to adopt a procedure radically different from that described above, as a result of the Church of Malta changing the form of the agape ceremony from a funeral one to one intended as a communal repast.

[5] Mgr. Vincenzo Borg and Mgr. Benedetto Rocco, "L'Ipogeo di Tac-Caghki a Malta", 1972.
[6] Enciclopedia Cattolica: Ente Per L.Enciclopedia Cattolica e per il Libro Cattolico Citta del Vaticano.

In the next room of this second catacomb an agape table, which is of a standard type for all Christian catacombs in Malta, was apparently cut out of the live rock soon thereafter, and the rest of the catacomb, both in its general form and the types of tombs in it, is typical of those of the early Christians. The agape table, as well as the others which were constructed in Maltese catacombs thereafter, consists of a round table some 3' in diameter with a raised rim except at the front where there is a concave opening; it is surrounded by a semicircular platform, usually about 2' above the floor and set within a half circle of live rock (figure 23).

The procedure for the celebration of the agape as a communal repast, at which a priest was present, and apparently held in a church, is described by Tertullian of Carthage when he wrote defending the rite in 197 in his Apologeticicus, chapter 39.

"Our dinner shows its idea in its name; it is called by the Greek name for love (agape). Whatever the cost, it is gain to spend in piety's name, for with that refreshment we help the needy . . . because with God there is greater consideration for those of lower degree. If the motive of the banquet is honest, take the motive as the standard of the other proceedings required by our rule of life. Since it turns on the duty of religion, it allows nothing vile, nothing immodest. We do not take our places at table until we have first tasted prayer of God. Only so much is eaten as satisfies hunger; only so much drunk as meets the needs of the modest.

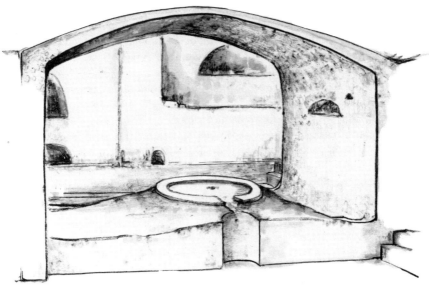

23. Agape Table and Platform

121

They satisfy themselves only so far as men will who recall that even during the night they must worship God; they talk as those would who know the Lord listens. After water for the hands come the lights; and then each, from what he knows of the Holy Scriptures or from his own heart, is called before the rest to sing to God; so that is a test of how much he has drunk. Prayer in like manner ends the banquet. Then we break up; but not to form groups for violence nor gangs for disorder, nor outbursts of lust; but to pursue the same care for self-control and chastity, as men who have dined not so much on dinner as on discipline".[7]

The agape apparently continued to be observed mainly as a communal repast in the churches of Carthage as evidenced by the fact that as late as 392 St. Augustine induced Bishop Aurelian of Carthage "to uproot those drunken feast in cemeteries", and stated "I wonder how such a pernicious error has crept in that they place food and wine on the corpses of the dead".[8]

In Italy, however, it appears that already toward the year 200 the term "refrigerare" was being used to refer to the semi-liturgical agape in honour of martyres. Such a ceremony was found to have been celebrated in the catacombs of St. Sebastian in Rome, which had a "triclinium",[8] i.e., banquet-chamber, containing a table-like couch, placed on three sides of a table, and used for reclining on at meals, which was the usual arrangement for the agape feast in Rome, Carthage, and Syracuse.

Moreover, the funerary character of the agape predominated again after 350 when the communal repast offered by the Church or rich Christians to the needy was transferred to large, charitable institutions, and the holding of the agape in basilicas and the serving of dinner in them except when required for the sake of hospitality, was prohibited, first by the Council of Laodicea in Frigia (about 360– 65), later by the Third Council of Carthage in 397, and subsequently by other councils up to as late as 692.[9]

Excluded from the churches, the agape continued to be celebrated in association with the cult of the dead as "refrigerum", a donation in suffragan.[9] This may account not only for the fact that the agape table became standard equipment in all catacombs in Malta where space permitted, but also explain why the agape table used in Malta, which is unique in the Christian world, retained what appears to be an obvious means of libation, i.e., the concave recess in front of the table against which a vase can be fitted in order to receive milk and wine poured upon the table, as had been done in former times upon the earth.

[7] Tertullian, Apologia de Spectaculis, Minucius Felix, translated into English by T. R. Glover, published by William Heinemann Ltd., London, 1953.

[8] Enciclopedia Cattolica: Ente Per L'Enciclopedia Cattolica e per il Libro Cattolico Citta del Vaticano.

[9] Enciclopedia Cattolica: Ente Per L'Enciclopedia Cattolica e per il Libro Cattolico Citta del Vaticano.

Eventually the holding of the agape in the catacombs was also prohibited by the ecclesiastical authority in Italy and Africa because of the abuses it gave occasion to and the pagan interpretation it could lead to.[9] This prohibition apparently was applied to Malta as well with the result that a number of agape tables were destroyed in Malta, such as in the catacombs of Bingemma, that in the funeral chapel in the intermediary level of St. Paul's Catacombs (figure 24), and on the right side of the entrance hall in the main catacomb of L'Abbatija tad-Dejr. Fortunately, however, most of these interesting and fine tables cut into live rock in the catacombs are still to be seen and afford silent evidence of the widespread practice of Christian funeral rites in Malta from the II century on.

Inscriptions, Frescos and Symbols

The crypt under St. Agatha's Church has on its walls a number of frescos and dedication crosses, and the vestibule and entrance hall of L'Abbatija tad-Dejr catacomb both have a number of inscriptions, frescos and symbols on their walls, but all of them are either known to have been or may well have been made many centuries after the catacombs were constructed.

Those within the catacombs proper, however, are all assumed to have been contemporary, it not being possible to establish anything to the contrary.

24. II–III Century Funeral Chapel

123

The inscriptions, frescos and symbols found within the various catacombs are remarkably few. This may have been due to the fact that, because of the persecutions, it was considered by all but a few that they could not run the risk of the tombs of their relatives being identified as Christian. Even after the persecutions ceased in the first part of the IV century, few of the catacombs appear to have contained inscriptions and symbols incised in their walls or on the tombs thereafter, but this may be because the construction of the catacombs was more or less completed in that century. Frescos were certainly painted in them from the IV century on but except for a few, there is little remaining of any of them, even those painted in the 15th century or later.

A list of the various inscriptions, frescos and symbols, divided according to whether they were found in Neo-Punic, Christian or Jewish catacombs, follows. As an indication of the century in which they may have been made, the type of tomb on which they appear or if not on a tomb, the types of tombs in the catacomb in which they appear are indicated.

Secondary School for Boys at Rabat: Neo-Punic inscriptions are placed over the five chambers within a room of that catacomb; each chamber contains five double tombs recessed into the wall, each of which has a low wall (4" high) at the outside edge of its floor but contains no fixtures, and has an undecorated three centred arch above.

Boys' School, Rabat: Christian, which, according to Eric Becker,[10] was an extension of a funeral club with tombs having square entrances recessed in barrel vaulted niches, and has a circled Greek cross on its side. This cannot be checked as the entrance was long ago covered up.

Main Catacomb at Salina, Christian: A symbol of a deer is incised on the wall behind the front door. On the wall at the rear of the centre passageway is a bas relief, apparently of Christ, and presumably with Peter and Paul. The catacomb has two tombs with window-like entrances, one of which is recessed in a barrel vaulted niche, while the other has a half dome niche above, and three saddleback tombs. On one of the latter are two circled Greek crosses (figure 25).

In a hole below a filed at Salina Catacombs; Christian: A monogram of Christ without a circle but with a lamb below it is incised on the side of an entrance to a tomb, recessed in the wall (figure 26). The tomb has a flat floor with a low wall on the outside edge and has a decorated arch across the top; it is otherwise similar to those in the original catacomb of the funeral club under the Secondary School for Boys at Rabat and may be late II century.

St. Thomas' Tower Christian Catacomb: Located on right side at end of first street in back of the tower: An inscription in Latin on a column on the side of the entrance of a tomb bears the most singular Christian inscription of any of the Maltese catacombs (figure 27). It is interesting that the letters standing for

[10] Eric Becker, "Malta Sotterranea". 1913 p. 50, pl. IV.

25. *Greek Cross in Salina Catacomb*

26. *Monogram of Christ with Lamb*

INNO
MINE
ÐMIΦHƧ
ƧORCEƧ
ETAMB
LAƧE
ÐNEƧΔ
LBVME
FΛC

27. *Latin Inscription*   28. *Monogram of Christ at Tad-Dejr Catacomb*

Christ Jesus are in Greek. There are six tombs in this catacomb, all of which are behind square window-like entrances recessed within a barrel vaulted niche.

St. Thomas Street corner of St. Pius V's Str, Rabat: Christian: A monogram of Christ is done in bas relief on a half dome niche above a window like entrance to a tomb, beside which is a Latin cross incised in the wall that is 2' high with a Greek cross at all three points.

Tal-Liebru; Christian; located $\frac{3}{10}$ths of a mile north of Ta' Gawhar Tower, on a hill to the left of the airport extension (545659): A monogram of Christ, several latin crosses, and a palm leaf are incised on the side of a number of tombs recessed behind a square window-like entrance within a barrel vaulted niche.

L'Abbatija tad-Dejr main Catacomb; Christian: A monogram of Christ is set into the centre of a design, like that in the Pantheon, in the ceiling of the fifth

29. *III Century Monogram of Christ*

tomb, a large canopy type, in the long row on the right extending from the entrance hall (figure 28).

L'Abbatija tad-Dejr minor catacomb to the right of the main one; dating possibly from the II century; Christian: To the left of the arch over the doorway leading to the inner chamber is a triple Greek cross. The tombs are mostly a Punic type with a window-like entrance, or are simple loculi and one is in the floor.

L'Abbatija tad-Dejr minor catacomb at the right end of the compound: Christian: The tombs are behind a square window-like entrance recessed within a wide barrel vaulted niche, one of which bore originally the following inscription: grego Rli (ac) dIONISii REPOSITA IN HOC (sepulchra) CORPORA.

Catacomb No 6; Christian; under Government nursery opposite St. Paul's Catacombs: A crude Greek Cross is cut through a screen wall to the right half way down the steps before the entrance room of the catacomb which contains a simple type of canopy tombs.

St. Agatha's Church III century Catacomb; Christian; There is a monogram of Christ on the side of a canopy tomb (figure 29). There are three frescos; two are on the side of canopy tombs, one representing a peacock and the other a wreath with ribbons etc. At the head of a canopy tomb, there is a fresco bearing an inscription in Greek. The catacomb also contains tombs with a window-like entrance recessed within a barrel vaulted niche or with a half dome shaped like a shell headed niche, and saddleback tombs.

St. Paul's Catacombs; Christian: At the far corner of the third cross row and the last passageway on the right is an inscription on the side of a canopy tomb, which had read EVITYXION (Eutychion) and next to it, but no longer visible, was a figure of a woman.

126

Jewish Catacombs: Located under Government nursery opposite St. Paul's Catacombs:

No. 12. On the wall at the foot of the stairs to the left of the original multiple tomb is an excellently incised menorah on a three legged stand (figure 30).

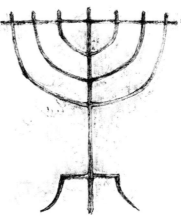

No. 10. Original: On the side of the frame around the entrance is a menorah. The tombs are recessed on either side of a passageway.

No. 10. Extension: A menorah is incised above the frame of a stone door on the right of the entrance room. There are two types of tombs, i.e., arcosoli which are sealed with tiles made of stone, and saddleback tombs, the tops of which were made separate.

No. 13. A menorah is incised above the doorway in front of the landing,

30. Menorah on Three Legged Stand

and at the end of a passageway leading off of a room to the left of the landing, a beautiful menorah is incised in the head end inside a tomb. The tombs are of different kinds but mostly arcosoli and canopy types.

No. 14. Above the entrance doorway at the foot of the steps is an incised menorah, and on the side of a free standing canopy tomb a diagram of a boat is incised as well as the name of a person in Greek (figure 31).

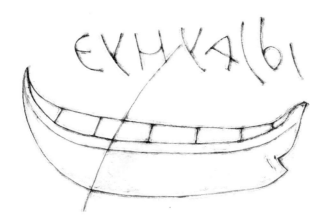

31. Boat and Greek Name on a Jewish Tomb

127

Jewish Catacomb under St. Agatha's Church: The original multiple tomb has an inscription above its window-like entrance of the names of persons in Greek, under which a menorah is incised in the wall. On the wall of the extended part of the catacomb, containing mostly Punic type tombs with window-like entrances recessed within barrel vaulted niches, is a palm leaf.

Types of Tombs and Niches

The catacombs described in detail under the section on Representative Catacombs are not only the most interesting and representative in Malta but they include those which are the most beautiful and spiritually impressive. This is due to the extraordinary art of those who created them and the skill of the fossors who cut them out of the live rock. Many of the catacombs are exemplary for their fine architectural designs in general but most extraordinary are the many types of tombs, which, over the first centuries of early Christianity in Malta, were developed into works of art.

The development of the different types of tombs that took place makes it possible, in conjuction with the sherds found in them, to identify in a general way the periods of origin and development of the different catacombs in which they are found. Some of the early types of tombs continued to be used along with those which were developed subsequently, but it appears nevertheless possible to recognize the approximate succession from the earliest types to the most developed except for two or three types which may have all been developed at about the same time.

The three principal factors, which appear to have influenced the adoption of the types of tombs used were first, the inheritance of the Punic and neo-Punic forms; second, the introduction of foreign forms, including Jewish, Roman and apparently Etruscan; and third, a gradual progression from the primitive to the most sophisticated and beautiful forms.

The original tombs found in the catacombs appear to be of four main types as follows:

1. The Punic type with a square window-like entrance placed in the wall some four feet above or level with the floor, which is recessed sideways generally or straight back, and has a flat floor with a low bank at one end into which two headrests are cut out, and a stilted arch niche measuring about 9″ × 9″ and 3″ deep in the rear wall.

2. A neo-Punic type with a square or rectangular window-like entrance placed in the wall some three feet above or level with the floor, which has either two tombs with a flat floor recessed on either side of a shallow trench or one tomb only at the side of a shallow trench, and a stilted arch niche in the rear wall.

3. A multiple tomb, traditionally Jewish, which is either a) a rectangular recess behind a square window-like frame in the wall, with a flat floor and a low

128

bank on one side with four or more headrests cut into it, or b) a rectangular entrance even with the floor with a shallow trench extending between two large rectangular recesses, each with a flat floor and a bank on one side with five or six headrests cut into it.

4. A rectangular chamber recessed behind a square or rectangular entrance a few inches off the floor with a passageway extending back between trough-like tombs recessed in the wall on either side and sometimes at the end, over which is a three centred arch some 2–3 feet above the low walls of the troughs.

The original Punic and neo-Punic types of tombs were subsequently modified in several ways. The first development was to recess the square entrance within a high relieving arch such as was used in the Etruscan catacombs. At about the same time the square entrance was placed within a barrel vaulted niche, which in turn was further modified at a later date, first by the addition of short columns on either side at the base, then the arch of the barrel vaulted niche was recessed in the form of a half dome and in a few instances the half dome was given the form of a shell headed niche (figure 32). In addition to the facade, a development took place also in the niche on an interior wall of the tomb; the first was the addition of small stilted arch niches 3″ wide, 3″ high and 2″ deep on one or both sides of the large stilted arch niche; then much later these small niches were cut into the wall

32. Punic Type Tomb with Shell Headed Niche

in such a way that they come to a peak at the top where it becomes flange with the wall.

Four types of tombs in addition to the foregoing, appear to be among the first to appear in Christian catacombs:

1. One is the loculus, a rectangular recess in the wall which was closed with a slab of stone placed upright and flange with the outer surface of the wall; it was usually small and was intended for babies and little children.

2. Another type, from which several others appear to have been developed, is a trough-like tomb level with the floor and with a foot high wall on all sides; these were constructed usually in series of two, three or four and were enclosed in a large recessed area some five feet high and about six feet wide. These tombs were closed by a stone or marble slab across their length, or by several square tiles, such as those used in Rome, but made of stone rather than earthenware.

3. A very early type of tomb is a double trough without a wall between, recessed lengthwise behind the outer wall and with a three centred arch above. It has a low bank at one end with two headrests, and between them and on either side is a small hole for holding a vase, while the floor of the trough is recessed several inches on either side of the centre as a drain for each body (figure 33).

4. The arcosolium type of tomb (figure 34) commonly seen in Roman catacombs but seldom in Malta, is similar to the one described just above, and probably came into use soon after. Instead of a three centred arch it has a semicircular arch lengthwise over the trough, which was closed with a single slab of

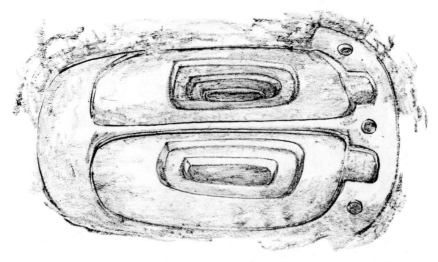

33. Floor of Early Type Tomb

34. Arcosolium Tomb

stone or stone slabs shaped into square tiles. The rear wall is sometimes cut in the shape of a half dome and more rarely as a wide shell headed niche.

The most developed and beautiful types of Christian tombs in Malta are the canopy and the saddleback described below.

1. From the trough-like tombs on the floor, it appears the canopy type tomb was gradually developed. Passageways were opened around two or three of them on as many sides, their outside walls were raised higher from the floor, and semi-circular arches were cut into the walls between the top of the trough and the ceiling. Subsequently, the troughs were combined into pairs, with or without a wall between them; they are raised off the floor and their side walls heightened accordingly (figure 35). The arches of some canopy tombs are decorated with scrolls in bas relief across both the long and short sides, and there are small columns on either side of the arch at its base. The floor inside the trough is flat with a low bank at one end and a recessed headrest for each body.

2. The saddleback, the most advanced type of all is found in both the small, family catacombs and the large ones of the Church; it is an improved canopy tomb, the cover for which is like the upper part of the Etruscan tombs and the Roman sarcophagi. In Italy, it is identified with a house, namely, the "home", but in Malta only as a saddleback (figure 36). In one Jewish catacomb, a double-pitched slab to cover each trough was made separate and then cemented on. Otherwise, however, the interior was cut out of the live rock and the double trough was hollowed out from below through an opening in the side or at one end. The interior, which sometimes is very large, has a low bank at one end with

131

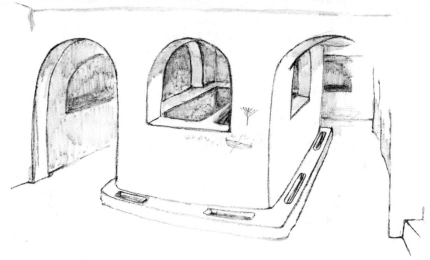

35. Canopy Tomb

36. Saddleback Tomb

132

two headrests recessed in it, and the floor may be recessed to provide a drain for each body. The opening on the side or end is generally square, and when the tomb is in use, it is closed by a block of stone and sealed with cement.

Representative Catacombs

The catacombs of Malta, of which there are several hundred, are found mostly to the south of the Melita ditch; this is due to the Roman law, which prohibited burials within the capital, and that elsewhere on the islands, there were no communities of any size. Of the 100–200 catacombs in the area adjoining the Melita ditch, all but three to four dozen have been built over and blocked. Among those remaining open for inspection, the most numerous are those of the funeral clubs or colleges, and the Jewish catacombs. Some of the largest catacombs belonged to the church, which in the II–III century gained ownership over various small catacombs belonging to the funeral clubs and families, and thereafter developed them into extensive complexes.

In Gozo, there is no corresponding concentration outside of the limits of Gaulus, and only a few catacombs have been identified elsewhere on the island.

In Malta, a considerable number of the earliest catacombs are located in remote parts of the island. Some belonged apparently to various religious groups, while others belonged to families, some of which resided on country estates.

The catacombs, described in the following thirteen numbered sections, have been selected as the most interesting and representative among both the small and the large. They are divided into two main groups. The first group is made up of those which were originally entered from the side of a hill, while those in the second were entirely subterranean and generally were constructed out from Punic or neo-Punic shaft/tombs. The first group was developed earlier on the whole than the second; several of the former have been identified by the sherds found in them as dating from the I century B.C. The second group appears to have begun with family catacombs, a number of which are found in the remote districts as well as adjoining the Melita ditch, and by the funeral clubs, all of which are in the Melita district. The Jewish catacombs likewise belong to the second group and all of them are also in the Melita area. Except for the four original Jewish tombs, three of which were multiple and date probably from the I–II century, the general layout of their catacombs and the types of tombs used in them are essentially the same as those of the Christian catacombs but for the absence of the agape table and the presence of a rectangular room without tombs, which was probably used for their religious rites. The catacombs, which belonged to the Church are all in the second group, and are all located in the Melita area; they appear to have been developed primarily during the II–IV century.

1. *Cave Catacomb Under Mosta Fort:* According to the types of tombs and niches found in this cave, it could be among the oldest of the catacombs described here and, although it appears from the sherds found in the tombs there, the families using it were converted to Christianity in about the II century, the tombs themselves remained unchanged. They were probably used by two or three neo-Punic families from the I century B.C. who may also have lived in the cave or nearby, and from the sherds found there, it appears that they continued in use until the V–VI century.

The cave is about 40' long and 20' wide and is recessed another 10' on the left and about the same on the right. There are seven separate tombs strung in a half circle from the side wall on the left and then along the rear wall out to the recess in the cave at the right end. Originally, the cave may not have opened out onto the side of the hill, which is directly above St. Catherine's chapel in Wied il-Ghasel, but instead was entered through a shaft from above which is to the rear on the left of the cave. There are now two entrances, one on either side of the central part of the cave, which appear to have been cut out of the side of the hill. There are several banks on the sides of the walls and what appears to have been a hearth is to the left of the entrance on the left, and, just inside the entrance is a Punic type stilted arch niche in the wall 9" wide, 7" high and 4" deep. There is also a niche in the wall behind the central part of the cave, which was probably for a lamp.

Tomb 1: This is at the back of the recessed area on the left. Its entrance is roughly cut into an irregular rectangle. Its interior is likewise roughly excavated and the floor is uneven. It is about 6' long, 4' wide and $4\frac{1}{2}$' high. At the rear is a crudely cut bank with two headrests recessed within a half dome niche. In the left wall near the back is a large Punic type niche, one side of which is uneven. There is also a niche in the right wall near the entrance but this was apparently for a lamp.

Tomb 2: The entrance to this tomb is likewise a roughly cut rectangle but there is a recess cut into the wall on three sides for placing a slab to seal the tomb. The tomb is placed sideways to the entrance. The walls curve in at the foot while at the head it is 5' wide and contains a low bank with two headrests within recess. The floor from the bank to the foot is 6'. In the rear wall is a large stilted arch niche about 20" wide, 19" high and 7" deep.

Tomb 3: This has a roughly cut rectangular entrance about 4' above the floor of the cave. The interior of the tomb is very rough. The tomb is about 5' wide and 4' to $4\frac{1}{2}$' high. A low bank at the head has two headrests cut deeply into it and is recessed within a half dome niche. The left wall is fairly straight but the right one curves inward at the foot.

Tomb 4: The entrance is behind a short passageway cut even with the floor and 3' to 4' wide. It appears the tomb had a slab recessed into the entrance to seal it. This tomb, which is the only late neo-Punic type in this catacomb

134

has a step below the entrance beyond which is a deep trench with a tomb on either side. The right one is 5' long, 3' wide and 3' to 4' high. It has a low bank without headrests. The tomb to the left is about the same size but the low bank is at the other end and apparently also without headrests. Above the trench, the ceiling is cut straight back, which gives the effect of a three centred arch above each of the tombs.

Tomb 5: The entrance to the tomb is behind the side of a bank 2' above the passageway leading to tomb 4. There is a suggestion of a barrel vaulted niche around the entrance which was cut back slightly to receive a slab to seal the tomb. The tomb, which is placed sideways to the entrance, is a little over 3' high and the floor is about 5' long and 4' wide. At the head end on the left is a low bank with headrests. In the rear wall is a stilted arch niche about 14" wide, 12" high and 5" deep at the base but is flange with the wall at the top. There is a smaller stilted arch niche in the right wall which is 8" wide, 7" high and 4" deep at the base and flange with the wall at the top.

Tomb 6: The entrance is even with a recess cut into the base of the wall. Although its opening is quite high, the tomb is quite small and irregular; it is less than 2' deep and $2\frac{1}{2}$' across.

Tomb 7: The entrance is in the corner of the cave on the right where a wall projects to the right. It is about 1' above a bank some 6" above the floor of the cave. A hole about 5" in diameter and 5" deep is in the left side of the bank which might have held a vase or amphora. The interior of the tomb is roughly cut; it measures 7' long, 4' wide and is 4' to $4\frac{1}{2}$' high. The floor is uneven and rises slightly at the rear and at the sides.

Recessed area at Right End of Cave: The wall on the right of tomb 7 is about 8' long and extending beyond it is a three quarters arch across the entrance to this area. Leading into the area is a short passageway cut even with the floor of the main cave. Although the left side of the recessed area extends out more than that on the right, it appears to conform essentially with the traditional semi-circular wall in the live rock surrounding the platform of an agape table. What was presumably an agape table has been entirely destroyed and in its place is a circular recess about 14" deep within the platform and even with the floor.

2. L'Abbatija tad-Dejr: The original tombs of this group of catacombs are located on the upper level at the back of the main catacomb. They are now badly destroyed but had been of a late neo-Punic type entered by deep shafts from the surface of a small field above the hill in which the main catacomb and three minor ones are recessed. At the basis of the shaft were tombs on either side, each with a trench between sections on either side for a body. In one of these shaft tombs, it was found that the tomb on the left had been broken into at the end and that the

135

trench between the two sections had been widened to make a passageway, thus rendering the sides too narrow to hold a body. The tomb on the right end of the shaft had remained undisturbed and it was in the trench between the two sections of that tomb that a small sherd was found that Professor Testini identified as I century A.D. "but not Christian", although he agreed it was not Punic. The other sherds found inside the upper area behind the main catacomb but not in a tomb, have been identified as types made and used during the following centuries: I century B.C.; I–II; I–III; and a whole group that appeared to have been a bowl, II–III. These sherds, of course, may indicate only the periods during which the upper level was frequented before or during whatever development may have taken place in the adjacent area below, and presumably before the main catacomb was placed in use. Another interesting find in the upper area was a heavy iron bracket with a large nail protruding from its side, indicating that a wooden coffin had been used in one of the tombs there.

Escarpment Catacombs: There are four catacombs behind an escarpment just to the left of the main catacomb. They are off the side of a field and are distributed unevenly along the length of the escarpment, which is about 100 yards. The first three catacombs were excavated within caves but the fourth, which is some distance beyond, was man-made throughout.

Cave 1: This catacomb is at the right end of the field, behind a low wall extending out from the escarpment; it contains only a small loculus inside to the left of the entrance, and behind a hole in the rear of the cave is a low recess but apparently no tombs have been recessed there although a number of sherds dating from the first centuries were found on the surface.

Cave 2: In front of this catacomb is a 10' wide area in the field on either side of which is a low wall. The catacomb has a large opening in the escarpment. In its left wall are two long loculi, one above the other; in the right wall are three tombs behind window-like entrances. At the far end of the three is one 7' long, 4' wide and $3\frac{1}{2}'$ high; in the centre is a small tomb only 1' wide, 2' long and 2' high; and the tomb near the entrance, which is a late neo-Punic type, has a trench 4' wide and 6' long, on either side of which is a tomb about 4' deep with a three centred arch over it. In the back is a further cave behind a low wall of modern stones; it is fallen in but in the left wall a window-like entrance can be seen with a small tomb behind about 4' long and 2' wide. In the wall on the right is a small loculus.

Cave 3: This catacomb has an entrance doorway about 5' high and 3' wide, in front of which is a low wall of modern stones on either side. Within the cave is a fairly large rectangular area with a concrete floor and to its right is a rather large semicircular cave. Behind the concrete floor is another cave with a trough-like tomb within its left wall. To the right in the floor of the cave is a very narrow tomb some 6' long. Above it is a natural bank beside the wall. In back of this cave is still another; in its back wall is a niche some 3' high, 3' wide and 4" deep. In the left wall of this inner cave is an open cave or tomb, and in its right wall is a tomb placed sideways behind a window-like entrance; its floor measures 6' from a low bank with two headrests on the right to a curved end at the foot, and it is 4' wide in the centre. Over the bank with headrests is a half dome recess 20" wide, 18" high and 6" deep. In the rear wall of this tomb is a square niche some 8" × 8" and 4" deep.

Man-Made Catacomb: This catacomb is some 100 feet beyond the group of three caves. It is divided by a straight passageway 3' wide and some 20' long, which curves at the end to the left slightly for another 3' to 4'. On the left of the passageway are three tombs, which from left to right are as follows:

Tomb A: It has a window-like entrance 22" × 27" recessed in a barrel vaulted niche. It is placed sideways with a floor 4' 10" long and 40" wide at the head but only 28" at the foot. A low bank at the right end has two headrests in it and is recessed within a half dome niche 35" wide, 25" high and 12" deep.

Tomb B: The window-like entrance is 21" × 22" and is recessed in a barrel vaulted niche. Its floor is 5' 1" long, and 39" wide at the head but narrows toward the foot to 32". There is a low bank at the right end with two headrests recessed within a half dome niche 34" wide, 20" high and 9" deep.

Tomb C: It is an arcosolium 5' wide, 31" high and 22" deep. Behind is another tomb with a window-like entrance which is hidden by a facade of rocks.

On the right side of the passageway from the rear to front are:

An Inner Cave: It contains a narrow passage 6' long cut even with the floor. On the left is a bank behind which is a tomb with a window-like entrance 23" × 25", recessed within an irregularly shaped barrel vaulted niche which is narrow at the top. The tomb, which is oval in shape, is 6' long and 51" wide at the centre. In the wall above the end of the narrow passage is another tomb with a window-like entrance 22" × 27" and 13" deep. A large, deep hole is in the rear wall near the top; it contained large pieces of a broken amphora, lined with cement, one of which had been previously broken and well mended. To the right of the narrow passage is a bank which recedes upward into the wall; there are several narrow crevices within the wall, behind which is an open space into which light from the outside shines.

Two Small Tombs in the Bank: One is 18" long, 8½" wide and 9" deep. The other a few inches to the right is 30" long, 12" wide but only 7" deep.

Loculus Tomb: High above the two small tombs, it is recessed 10" in the wall and measures 26" × 11" with a frame around its sides to receive a slab to enclose it.

Semicircular Recess: It is at the front of the main passageway and

137

closed off from the outside by a new stone wall; it is 6' 4" wide, 5' 6" deep and 40" high and stands about 2' above the floor.

A number of sherds were found in the tombs and caves of these catacombs, all of which have been identified as belonging to the Christian era. All but one could be definitely dated at from the II–III century; the exception dates possibly from late in the I century, although it is a type that was used also in the II–III. In view of the proximity of these four catacombs to the late neo-Punic area described above, they appear to afford the earliest evidence of Christian catacombs on the island of Malta.

Catacombs Recessed in the Hill: The hill of solid rock sloping down from the field where the late neo-Punic shafts come to the surface, no doubt once extended out beyond where the dirt road is some 50' in front of what is now a stone facade 15' high that runs some 100' across the courtyard, formerly occupied by a Byzantine basilica, extending from a small chapel on the left to where the slope extends out to the road at the right end. The entrance with a large, iron gate next to the small chapel, is to the main catacomb. To its right is a large hole in the facade where there are two large tombs and three loculi, and beyond to the right is a small catacomb. A fourth is at the front, right corner.

Tombs Behind a Hole in the Facade: These tombs, which appear from their primitive type to be the oldest within the slope of the hill, are recessed in the wall on either side of a wide passageway, which originally may have been entered by a shaft. The tomb on the left is about 6' long, 4' wide and 3' high and placed about 2' above the floor. Its floor is flat except at the outside edge where there is a low wall. The tomb on the right is about the same size; its floor is almost even with the passageway and it has no wall at its outside edge. In the side wall above the tomb are three small loculi.

Catacomb Behind a Recessed Landing: A wide landing with three steps at the front leads to a rectangular doorway. In the wall on the right of the landing is a small Punic type, single tomb, which may have been reached by a shaft before the hill was excavated at the front. Extending from the doorway is an $8\frac{1}{2}'$ wide passageway 13' long on either side of which is a large semicircular platform on both of which there may have once been an agape table. In the circular wall of live stone around the platform on the left are two small loculi, while in the wall behind the platform on the right are three tombs. That at the left end is a Punic type, double tomb with a window-like entrance and a standard oven type interior 5' long and $3\frac{1}{2}'$ wide with a curved recess at either end and a low bank with two headrests on the right.

The tomb in the centre has a window-like entrance with a half dome niche above and short columns on either side at the front. The oven shaped tomb, which is placed sideways, is 5' long and 2'2" wide. It has a curved recess at the foot and a shallow one at the head behind a low bank with a headrest.

138

At the right end of the wall is a single, small tomb behind a window-like entrance with a half dome niche above. The tomb is oven shaped, $4' \times 2\frac{1}{2}'$ with a low bank and headrest at one end.

At the end of the passageway is a large, arched doorway; incised in the wall above it to the left is a triple Greek cross joined horizontally with a small cross on top of the centre one, while in the wall to the right is a large, single Greek cross. Running crossways behind the arched doorway is a 4' wide corridor, 13' long and 7' high. Along the back wall is a 1' high curb and beside it at the left end is a 6' long, narrow tomb in the floor. In the wall at the right end are two small loculi and at the left end in the near wall is a loculus 16'' wide and $5\frac{1}{2}''$ deep with a headrest in a low bank at one end.

In the back wall, opposite the arched doorway and about 3' above the floor is a large tomb. It has a window-like entrance recessed within a barrel vaulted niche. Its floor is flat, 6' long and 4' wide and without a bank or headrest. The right wall contains a semicircular niche some $3\frac{1}{2}'$ high and 4'' deep; the left wall also contains a similar but somewhat shallower niche.

Catacomb With an Agape Table: At the right end of the courtyard is the entrance to a most lovely, small catacomb probably dating from the II-III century. Until the end of the last century according to an 1898 illustration,[11] this catacomb was entered from above by a neo-Punic shaft; in fact, the sides of the entrance still contain in the live rock the original holes for the toes, which is typical for all neo-Punic shafts. A wide passageway extends down the centre of the catacomb, on the left of which is a well preserved agape table about $2\frac{1}{2}'$ above the floor and surrounded by a semicircular platform set within a half circle wall of live rock. Within the wall in back of the agape are two tombs with window-like entrances recessed in barrel vaulted niches. On the right of the passageway, opposite the agape table, is a wall with high arches and behind it is an open rectangular space some eight feet wide. At the back are several tombs in the wall, all but one of which are exceptional in that the window-like entrance is within an unusually wide barrel vaulted niche; it was over one of these that an inscription had been painted in Latin. At the end of the centre passageway, beyond the arched wall, is a single tomb recessed in the right wall.

The Main Catacomb: Behind the large, iron gate at the left end of the facade by the courtyard which was undoubtedly cut out of the hill some centuries later than the catacombs, was one of the most beautiful and best laid out catacombs in Malta but now in a poor and neglected state. Across the front of the catacomb is a large rectangular area which originally may have contained an agape table and platform on the right if not on both sides, but which are no longer visable. In the back of it is a wall with arches, behind which are passages

---

[11] A. A. Caruana, "Ancient Pagan Tombs and Christian Cemeteries", 1898.

between two rows of canopy tombs directly to the rear and short rows of canopy and/or arcosoli tombs on the sides. Above and to the sides of the arches, various symbols and crosses have been incised, the dates of which are possibly much later than the catacomb.

Among the two rows of large canopy tombs, each containing about eight, the fifth in the right row has a most beautiful ceiling with a fine design in the centre of which is a monogram of Christ (figure 28). Diagonally opposite this tomb is another which has a scroll in low bas relief across the long arch in front. In the wall of live rock on the right of the catacomb, an arcosolium tomb has been excavated which has a beautiful and exceptionally wide shell headed niche over the top (figure 34).

Only three sherds were found in the canopy tombs of the main catacomb; their dates have been identified as from the IV to VI century during which time the catacomb was certainly in use but its construction may well have been completed before the reign of peace began in 330.

3. Bingemma: It appears that in about the I century B.C. a group of devout and courageous people, who could no longer tolerate the imposition of religious beliefs by the Romans, sought refuge in the caves alongside the upper part of the ravine at Bingemma Gap; they formed a hermit like colony that remained there for some 400 years, some of whom may have continued on in the caves until the VII–VIII centuries.

Farther down the ravine they cut out catacombs into the hard coralline rock, each with a number of tombs for their dead. As this colony was apparently left to its own resources and was never persecuted for its religious beliefs by the Romans, the entrances into their catacombs, which open out onto the side of the hill, were not hidden nor blocked up. These catacombs are traditionally called the "caves of the Jews", i.e., Gherien-el-Lhwwd, but the term Lhwwd was also used to mean "foreigners". Strangely enough a number of the entrances to those catacombs, opening out in the lower part of the hill, resemble those of the Etruscans as they are recessed within a high relieving arch (shown on the cover) and a number of the entrances to individual tombs within the catacombs are likewise recessed. However, the original tombs there appear to be quite typical of the kinds used by the Punics and the neo-Punics after them.

The lower part of the hill, in which catacombs were apparently first excavated, is between a ledge forming several fields, just above the channel of the ravine, and another ledge some 50–60 feet above. The higher catacomb area opens out onto the upper ledge. The tombs are recessed at the back of two large open caves, and within a large facade in the wall of the hill. One is on the left where a path leads to the top of the hill. In all, there are about 50 tombs in this upper area, but unlike those in the area below, they are too destroyed to survey effectively and, due to their exposed location, no sherds were found in them that can

140

be relied upon for evidence of the periods in which they were excavated and used. In the lower part of the hill there are 15 catacombs opening out onto or just above the lower ledge; these contain a total of 53 tombs. Distributed unevenly on several levels just above them, but below the upper ledge, are seven more catacombs containing another 23 tombs, thus making 22 catacombs with 76 tombs in all. As these catacombs and tombs are almost all in their original state, a complete survey would be useful, but for the purposes of this introductory analysis of the catacombs, four of the most representative, together with what appears to have been a chapel, are described in detail below:

Catacomb 1: At the right end, above the ledge forming a field above the channel of the ravine and located beside the Victoria Lines viaduct, which separates the catacomb area from the cave dwellings, a low doorway is located on the side of the hill some six feet up. Inside is the "vestibule" of the catacomb; it is over 6' high, covering a horseshoe shaped area of about 12' × 10'. The arched composition of the ceiling and the barrel vaulted niche in which the entrance to the tomb on the left is set, above a 16" bank, make a fine composition (figure 37). At the right end of the "vestibule" is a chamber for two tombs (A and B), the rectangular entrance of which has a high relieving arch in the wall.

Tomb A: is placed to the left of a shallow trench 22" wide and extending almost the length of the tomb which is 5' 8". Across the head of the tomb at the back is a bank 6" high and 6" wide but without headrests. At that end the tomb is 46" wide but at the foot, which curves inward at the back, it is

37. Bingemma Catacomb

141

only 36″. The recess above the floor of the tomb is about 3′ high; the three walls all curve inward slightly toward the top. About 4″ from the edge of the floor bordering the trench is a shallow drain and there is a further short drain crossing it about 2′ from the bank at the back. On the floor of this primitive tomb a half bowl was found, which has a folded lip at the top and is made of yellow pottery speckled with red dots, that dates from the I century A.D. Professor Testini of the Institute of Christian Archaeology at the University of Rome stated, however, that it was "not Christian", but then added "possibly not Christian".

Tomb B: is recessed sideways behind tomb A. It has a semicircular recess in the wall at its head on the left, in front of which is a bank 8″ wide and 6″ high across the tomb which is 38″ wide. The length of the floor from the edge of the bank is 5′, and the height of tomb above the floor is 30″. Three sherds of different types found in the earth covering the tomb floor have been identified as Christian, dating from the II–III century, and a fourth has been identified only as being later than I century.

Tomb C: which is the one on the left of the "vestibule", described above, is placed sideways to its entrance; it is only 40″ long but 44″ in width, and about 3′ high. It contained several Christian type sherds identified at II–III century and a piece of a greenish glass bowl of the III century from Syria.

Tomb D: is opposite the entrance to the "vestibule"; it has a small, arched opening in the wall, which may have been sealed originally by a stone now lying outside the catacomb that has a rectangular plug extending from its back similar to those used by the funeral clubs but not so pronounced. The tomb is a late neo-Punic type which, however, continued to be used by Christians. It has a trench 22″ wide extending back 6′ from the entrance to the entrance of tomb E behind. On either side of the trench is a double tomb 33″ wide; each of them has a low bank 6″ wide across its near end with two headrests. Five Christian types of sherds were found in this tomb, all of which have been identified as II–III century.

Tomb E: is entered by an arched opening which is quite wide and is recessed within a barrel vaulted niche. The tomb is placed sideways and is about 63″ long and 32″ wide; across its head on the right is a low bank with two headrests, one of which is quite small. Recessed in the rear wall is a typical Punic stilted arch niche 15″ wide and 10″ high.

Catacomb II: A short distance to the left of Catacomb I, beyond the entrance to two other catacombs, is the entrance to this catacomb a few feet above the field. It is a fairly large catacomb, having a central passageway 6′ high and 3′ wide and extending back 25′. On the right is first a large semicircular recess measuring 12′ 4″ across the front and 5′ 2″ deep at its centre, which is typical of those in which an agape table and platform were usually placed. Unfortunately, however, it has been destroyed and no longer definitely recognizable as an agape table. Sherds found on the platform were identified as Christian and from the II–IV centuries. Within the semicircular wall there is but one tomb (A) which is placed on the left.

Tomb A: has a rectangular window-like entrance, to the right of which the wall is cut out in the form of a right angle, and on its left is a small niche, apparently for holding a lamp. A trench 20" wide extends 67" back from the entrance to a low bank. To the right of the trench is a tomb 47" wide, 6' 2" long and 31" high. At its near end is a low bank with two headrests.

Tomb B: is across from the semicircular platform and just to the left of the outside doorway. Its window-like entrance, which is 31" above the floor, 22" high and 21" wide, and recessed in a barrel vaulted niche. The tomb is placed sideways and measures 63" in length and 44" in width. Across its right end is a low bank with two headrests behind which is a half dome niche 29" high. To the right of the entrance to this tomb is a large half dome niche, below which is a bank 28" long. Within the centre of the bank is a shallow hole some 5" in diameter which may have been intended to hold a low emphora or possibly the tabernacle of the Eurcharist.

Tomb C: is to the right of the large half dome niche. Its window-like entrance is 24" × 20", recessed within a barrel vaulted niche, and placed about 3' above the floor of the passageway. The tomb is a late neo-Punic type with a trench 28" wide, 1' or more deep, and 6' 6" long. On its right is a tomb 6' long and generally 43" wide as there is a slight curve in the rear wall. Across its far end is a low bank with two headrests. On the left of the trench is a tomb 48" wide, 6' 6" long and 30" high. The floor is flat without a bank.

The central corridor, which extends beyond the "vestibule" at the front by $12\frac{1}{2}$', is lined with three tombs on either side. Each tomb has a window-like entrance recessed within a barrel vaulted niche.

Tomb D: is the first on the right; its entrance is 26" × 20" and is only about 1' above the floor of the corridor. A narrow trench extends 63" from the entrance. On its left is a tomb about 5' wide with a low bank across the rear with two headrests. A stilted arch niche some 9" × 9" is in the wall on the left and another of the same size is in the wall on the right of the trench.

Tomb E: is to the left of tomb D, where the corridor narrows slightly, and is about 40" off the floor. It is placed sideways and measures 6' long and 42" wide. Across its right end, which is concave, is a low bank with two headrests. The foot end is also concave. Recessed in the rear wall is a regular Punic type stilted arch niche about 9" × 9" and on either side of it is a small niche having the same form as the larger one.

Tomb F: is at the end of the corridor on the right, and is about 3' off the floor. It is placed sideways and is 69" long and 41" wide, both ends of which are concave. Across the right end is a low bank with two headrests, and

143

a small hole in it probably to hold a low vase or amphora. On its wall at the rear is a Punic type stilted arch niche some 9" × 9" with a small one on its left the top of which comes to a peak more or less flange with the surface of the wall.

Tomb G: is the first one on the left of the extended corridor and is only about 1' above its floor. A trench 23" wide extends 6' from the entrance to a small step and a bank behind it; the total length is 6' 8". On its right is a tomb 43" wide across the rear end in which there is a low bank with two headrests.

Tomb H: is the next on the left where the corridor begins to narrow slightly. Its entrance is 40" off the floor. It is placed sideways and its plain, flat floor is 65" long and 41" wide. In its rear wall, which is 29" high, is a Punic type stilted arch niche some 9" × 9", on either side of which is a small niche the top of which comes more or less to a peak even with the surface of the wall.

Tomb I: is the last on the left of the corridor; its entrance is 2' off the floor. It is placed sideways and the walls on either end are concave. It is 70" long overall and 42" wide. In front of the semicircular recess in the wall on the left is a low bank with two headrests. On the rear wall is a Punic type stilted arch niche about 9" × 9" and to its right is a somewhat smaller but similar one.

Catacomb III: is reached by steps cut in the side of the stone surface of the hill above a field just to the left of a low rubble wall dividing it from the field where catacombs I and II are located. The entrance to this catacomb is notable for its high relieving arch, the inside of which has acquired an orange-brown colour above the rectangular entrance 30" wide. A further unusual feature of the entrance is the post hole on either side, apparently used to close the catacomb as was done in the Copper Age temples. The most important feature of this catacomb is its agape table and surrounding platform on three sides set within a semicircular walled recess; the agape table is primitive but definitely recognizable for what it is.

A passageway 42" wide extends from the entrance for 10'. To its right is the platform of the agape, 9' long and 9' 4" deep in the centre; on either end it curves inward until coming to the agape table which protrudes forward in a semicircle. The table is 40" in diameter on the outside and within a partially destroyed 4" rim, it measures an uneven 32". At the front, the rim is open and a narrow channel leads from it to the floor of the passageway. Above the passage-way is a three centred arch across the length of the agape platform. At the left end of the platform is a 2' projection of the wall 10" high. In the wall in back of the centre of the agape platform is a large niche about 9" × 9" and on the right is a smaller one 4" at the base which comes to a peak 5" above. There is also a small niche on the left of the large one which is also about 5" high but it is wider across the top than at the base. The wall to the right of the agape platform is

144

broken through and a destroyed tomb can be seen extending back of it. On the opposite side of the passageway from the agape platform is the only existing tomb in this catacomb.

The tomb is recessed behind a window-like entrance, recessed within a barrel vaulted niche about 2' above the floor of the passageway. The left side of the niche is cut out apparently to secure a stone slab to seal the tomb. In the wall above it is a small niche resembling a keystone measuring 4" across and 5" high. Extending from the entrance is a deep trench 20" wide and 54" long at the head of which is a low bank 9" wide. The tomb which is on the right, is 68" long and 42" wide; at its near end is a low bank 9" wide with two headrests. In the wall above the foot of the trench is a small niche 6" × 5" and 4" deep.

Two sherds were found near the agape table; one has been identified as I century B.C. and the other as II–III A.D. Within the tomb, four sherds of primitive, home-made pottery were found, all of which have been identified as III–IV century. One piece consisted of part of the side and base of a low bowl, and another was also part of the side and base of a bowl which had been decorated with two rows of small circles by pressing the edge of a small cylindrical article against it. These primitive pieces of pottery might indicate that those who made them had been more or less cut off from the rest of the island.

Catacomb IV: Is located up to the left of Catacomb III and can best be entered through a large room above it which is just under the upper ledge; the floor to the left of this room is broken and a ramp leads down to the catacomb. This large room, which is about 17' long, 10' 9" wide and over 6' high, may have been used for the funeral rite as there are no tombs recessed within its walls and the wall on the left, which is semicircular in shape, suggests it may have once contained an agape table and platform. That the floor in front of it on the left is broken, might have occurred accidently during the destruction of what had been an agape table.

The ramp is just at the end of a 19' corridor, which is 41" wide and 67" high. The doorway at the other end opens out onto the side of the hill; it is 27" wide and likewise 67" high. Inside the catacomb on the right of the doorway is what appears to have been an agape table and platform which at some time was largely destroyed. It is surrounded by the traditional, semicircular recess in the wall of live rock. The platform beside the passageway is 10' 9" and 7' 4" deep at the centre. In the wall behind the platform are several small niches for lamps. The recess above the platform is 51" high and is arched across the front.

There are three tombs in this catacomb; two are opposite the "agape" platform and the third is at the end of the corridor and to the right of where the ceiling is broken through.

Tomb A: is to the left of the doorway to the outside. It has a window-like entrance 24" high and 23" wide, recessed in a deep barrel vaulted niche

25" above the floor. The tomb is placed sideways and is 68" long up to a 9" wide low bank with two headrests recessed in a half dome niche 21" high. The width of the tomb at the centre is 45" but narrower at the ends. Above the foot end on the right is a large stilted arch niche 16" wide and 14" high, which is recessed in such a way that it forms a half dome, the top of which is flange with the surface of the wall.

Tomb B: to the right of tomb A, has a window-like entrance 29" high and 21" wide, recessed in a barrel vaulted niche 38" wide, 37" high and 10" deep. A semicircular niche is recessed into the left side of its wall. Extending back from the entrance is first a low $8\frac{1}{2}$" bank, followed by a trench 46" long and 18" wide. On either side is a tomb, the back wall of which is slightly concave. The tomb on the right is 46" long up to a low bank with two headrests and 55" wide in the centre. In the rear wall above the centre is a large stilted arch niche 24" × 15". The tomb on the left of the trench is 56" long and 44" wide at the centre and its floor is flat without a bank at one end.

Tomb C: which is partly hidden from view by the ramp, has a window-like entrance 17" high and 16" wide, with a recess on either side to receive a slab to seal the tomb, and the whole is recessed within a barrel vaulted niche $30\frac{1}{2}$" wide and 17" deep. Within its wall on the left is a niche 14", wide and 9" high. The tomb is placed sideways and measures 67" long, 38" wide at the right end where there is a low bank with two headrests, and 35" across at the foot. Both ends of the tombs are concave, and that above the head end contains a niche 16" wide and 10" high.

Among the sherds found in a trench cut into the passageway at the edge of the "agape" platform was one which has been identified as I–II century and another as late II century. In addition, a number of sherds were found there which appear possibly to have been medieval, which would suggest that during and after the Arab occupation of Malta, a group of refugees may have lived in this area and used this catacomb for the burial of their dead.

Enlarged Cave Resembling a Chapel: At the end of the field on the left where the hillside bends to the west, is a large doorway lined on either side with heavy, stone blocks. Inside is a large area excavated in the live rock, measuring 27' from front to rear, 20' across and over 8' high. High in the back wall toward the right side is a large stilted arch niche some 2' × 2' and about 6" deep within which a second niche about 1' × 1' can be made out. The rear, left corner of the area is roughly semicircular and within it appears to have been a platform, in the centre of which may have been an agape table. Below this platform at a slightly lower level, is an area about 4' wide stretching from wall to wall and in the centre at the far end is a hearth with a low rim around it except by the wall. Sloping down to the level of the floor, its outer edge reaches the wall just below the large niche, while at the near end it extends to a recess cut into the side wall. At the back of the semicircular wall is a niche measuring about 10″ × 10″ and about 5″ deep.

Diagonally opposite from the area described above and just around to the right from the doorway is also a semicircular area within which is a raised platform that could likewise have contained a smaller agape table.

This rather extraordinary layout suggests strongly that this large recessed room, excavated into the side of the hill, could well have been a chapel attended by early Christians from possibly the end of the II century.

4. *Salina Catacombs:* They include a group of four small catacombs which were originally entirely recessed within a low hill of stone sloping down to an open field, and three individual chambers with one or two tombs each. Three of the small catacombs now surround the sides of an open rectangle bordering the field. The rectangle was cut into the hill probably in the IV–V century or later to allow access to the three catacombs. Originally, there were some tombs recessed in the part of the hill which was cut away; the outline of several large loculi, which had been located high up on the right, as well as some tombs that had been recessed in the floor, can still be seen. Among the sherds found in this recessed area between the three small catacombs is one which has been identified as I–II century; the others have been identified as from the II–III, IV–V and V–VI.

The small catacomb on the left of the recessed area is, except for the door leading into it and a break over the lower area, still recessed entirely in the hill where it continues out to the edge of the field. This catacomb appears to have been the first, both from the sherds found there, which have been identified as as II–III and III–IV centuries, and from the improved type of trough-like tombs contained in it; they are made up of groups of three or four with three centred arches above the three sides having passageways around them, while the fourth side is in the live rock.

The middle catacomb, which is recessed within the hill behind a window cut into the live rock, contains a more developed type of tomb, indicating a stage in the transition from the trough-like groups to the independent canopy tombs. They are surrounded by passageways on three sides and the sides of the tombs are higher than the trough-like type.

The catacomb on the right is entered through a door below some steps and is recessed entirely within a slope of the hill extending out to the field. It is a later type of Christian catacomb, having an agape table surrounded by a semicircular platform behind which are several examples of a free standing canopy tomb (figure 35).

The fourth small catacomb is located behind a wooden doorway about 100′ to the left of the recessed area. The key is kept at the farmhouse on the opposite side of the road and about 200′ up from the chapel of Annunciation. The entrance, which may originally have been recessed vertically into the hill, is below several steps; the catacomb is entirely recessed into the hill. A passageway extends to the rear wall some 20′ behind. On the left is an agape table surrounded by a semicircular platform raised about 2′ above the floor and within what had been a half circle wall; subsequently its right side was cut away level with the floor to make room for a tomb At the front of the agape table, there is a concave recess to receive a vase and on either side of it is a small seat. The ceiling above the platform gives evidence of having been raised and only the top of a barrel vaulted niche remains. To the left in back of the agape table is a tomb with a window-like entrance recessed within a barrel vaulted niche and to its right is one with a window-like entrance above which is a half dome niche. Around to the right of the door is another such tomb.

The rest of the catacomb is quite advanced in its architecture and the whole composition is no doubt the most beautiful of any of the catacombs of Malta. There are three saddlebacks; that beside the agape platform has been left unfinished against the side wall (figure 36); the others on the right stand entirely free but the far one is also unfinished. Three sherds, which were found in the rear tomb, have been identified as II–III century; II–III–IV; and V century, the third indicating probably only that the catacomb was still used in that century. This tomb is notable for the scrolls across its arches and the Greek cross within a circle, which is done in bas-relief on two sides (figure 25). The near saddleback has a remarkable frond design on the front (figure 38).

In the wall at the end of the central passage-way is a design about 3′ high placed about 3′ above the floor, which is now coated with mud but may be of Christ and possibly Peter and Paul. Behind the entrance door is a crudely incised figure of an animal which may represent a deer or lamb.

In the field in front of the fourth catacomb is a hole leading down to a short passageway on the right of which is an open rectangular recess, about 1′ above the floor, which may have once been a primitive type tomb. On the left is a tomb recessed in the wall about 3′ above the floor; it is about 6′ long, 3′ high and it has a low wall along its front. There is a low relief scroll across its arched facade and on the left column is an incised design, which at its base extends down to a monogram of Christ with a figure of a lamb below it (figure 26). At the end of the short passageway and high up on

38. *Frond Design on Salina Tomb*

148

the wall to the right is a square entrance, now blocked, that may have led to the catacomb in back.

5. *St. Thomas/St. Pius V's Sts. Catacombs:* There are six catacombs and/or caves at the corner of the above streets in Rabat. Within the centre of the area is recessed a rectangular garden surrounded by an escarpment on two sides. Originally, a low hill probably extended over the whole area. Apparently it contained several caves open to the outside while vertical shafts may have provided entrances into the man-made catacombs. The catacombs and/or caves appear to have been put into use in succession from the far left corner around to the right corner on the near side.

1. The first, which is on the far left corner, appears to have been a natural cave without any tombs having been recessed into its walls.

2. The next is to the right and contains a late neo-Punic type of tomb with two sections recessed in the walls on either side of a shallow trench. In the rear wall is a Punic type, stilted arch niche about 9″ × 9″ and 4″ deep.

3. At the corner between the two sides of the escarpment is a cave; it contains a single, rectangular tomb recessed in the wall on the left about 3′ above the floor. In the wall on the right is a double tomb, which has a low bank with two headrests at one end and is recessed within a half dome niche.

4. In the centre of the long escarpment on the right is a high arched doorway, behind which are two rectangular rooms. There is nothing in the second but the first contains a Punic type double tomb recessed in its left wall. At one end of the tomb is a low bank with two headrests, and in its rear wall is a large niche with a small one beside it.

5. Farther to the right in the long escarpment a chamber contains, behind a window-like entrance, recessed within a barrel vaulted niche, two double tombs; one is recessed in the wall on the right and the other at the back.

6. At the corner on the right is a rectangular door, behind which is a flight of steps leading to a catacomb with a long corridor. In the right wall are two exceptionally beautiful and interesting tombs. Both are placed sideways behind a window-like entrance above which is a half dome niche. They both have short columns on either side in front, placed flange with the outer surface of the wall, while the window-like entrance is behind. The width across the front of the first tomb is 54″ while that of its window-like entrance is only 21″. In the centre of the half dome niche above the rim of the entrance is a bas relief of a monogram of Christ with a barely discernible Greek cross and the letters alpha and omega. On the wall to the right of the entrance to this tomb is a 2′ Latin cross with a Greek cross at all three points. The interior of the tomb is 6′ long in front but as the rear wall is slanted inward at the foot, it is only 5′. The width is 6′ and it is 4′ high. At the head end is a low bank with two headrests cut deep

into it, which is recessed in a half dome niche 3′ 6″ high. In the rear wall is a large Punic type niche 15″ wide and 10″ high.

Between the first tomb and the second is a large niche 30″ wide at the base with a trough 6″ wide and 4″ deep across it.

The width at the front of the second tomb is somewhat less than that of the first but otherwise it is the same except that the upper part of the window-like entrance has been hollowed out. The interior of the tomb is 6′ long, 5′ wide and 4′ high. At the left end is a low bank with two headrests cut deep into it, which is recessed within a half dome niche 3′ high.

In the wall on the left side of the corridor there is only an arched recess which apparently was intended to be another tomb but never excavated.

6. Ghar Gerduf: In Gozo, only two catacombs have been definitely identified, although there appears to be one under the hill opposite Ghar Gerduf and one at the so-called "cemetery" beside the road at Wardija, both of which have not been investigated due to their present condition. The only catacomb identified beside Ghar Gerduf is in a ledge above two fields in back of Obajjar where the road from Marsalforn running behind Qolla s. Safra, turns north. This catacomb appears to have had a number of large loculi placed on either side of a passageway, which was destroyed by tunnelling from one side of the ledge to the other, and as a result nothing as to its layout, et cetera can be determined.

The catacomb at Ghar Gerduf, which was originally excavated into the side of a hill, has also been tunnelled from one end to the other to make a shed for hay, etc., but some dozen tombs can be identified. Several are around to the left and the others are recessed in the wall on either side high above the tunnelled area. They are much like some of the tombs excavated in the island of Malta during the same period, which, according to a sherd found in one of them, is the II–III century. They have a flat floor with a low bank at the head with headrests and a large Punic type stilted arch niche in the rear wall, beside which is a similar but smaller one.

7. Mosta Fort: This is a small catacomb which was used apparently by a family that converted a neo-Punic shaft/tomb by elongating the shaft into a corridor and extending it a bit back to install steps. It is one of the best examples of the transformation of such a tomb into a catacomb with early Christian type tombs and an agape table. On the right end of the original shaft is the neo-Punic tomb behind a rectangular entrance 40″ high and 30″ wide. The tomb is 3′ long, 2′ wide and about 3′ high.

A high, rectangular doorway with a relieving arch in the live rock above it leads to two steps and down into the 6′ high corridor. It is $2\frac{1}{2}$′ wide and about 20′ long and toward the rear is only 5′ high. A tomb recessed in the wall immediately to the right may have been the first; it has a window-like entrance 27″ high and 22″ wide, recessed within a barrel vaulted niche. The tomb, which is placed sideways, is about 5′ long and 3′ wide. It has a low bank on the left with two headrests and the wall behind is semicircular. The floor of the tomb is flat and only slightly curved at the foot. The first tomb on the left of the corridor has a window-like entrance recessed within a barrel vaulted niche. It is placed sideways and its floor is 5′ long and $2\frac{1}{2}$′ wide, and at the right end is a low bank with two headrests. The centre of the floor contains a rectangular recess about 3′ long on either side of a central rib, and each recess is bordered by a double frame cut in the live rock. The left end has a semicircular recess in the wall. In the rear wall, which is about 3′ high, is a stilted arch niche 9″ wide, 9″ high and 3″ deep. Farther on the left side of the corridor, a second tomb is recessed lengthwise in the wall; there is a rectangular recess with a three centred arch 3′ high above the level of the tomb wall; and the tomb, which is 6′ long and 3′ wide is recessed 3′ deep behind a wall separating it from the corridor. There is a 5′ semicircular niche in the rear wall and in the wall at each end is a semicircular niche about 20″ wide, 18″ high and 6″ deep. Within the large niche in the rear wall is a Punic type stilted arch niche 9″ wide, 9″ high and 3″ deep. The floor of this tomb contains two long recesses curved at the ends, on either side of the centre rib (figure 33). At the right end of the tomb floor is a low bank with two headrests and between them and on either side is a small hole for a vase.

On the right side of the corridor and at its end opposite the tomb described just above, is a large, rectangular recessed area with curved corners some 8′ wide and 6′ deep on the right side but somewhat less on the left. There is a three centred arch 4′ above the base of the recess which is about 2′ above the floor of the corridor. An agape table $3\frac{1}{4}$′ feet is in the centre, the edge of which is even with the side of the corridor. The usual platform surrounding the agape on three sides, however, is not traditional, not only because the area is not a half circle but also it slants sharply downward on the right toward the rear, which might indicate that it was not designed to serve as a couch for guests at a feast but rather was more symbolical than practical and probably meant more for libation purposes than for a "communal repast".

8. *Funeral Club Catacombs:* Many of these catacombs have been destroyed, blocked up or otherwise made no longer available for inspection. Of those remaining that have been identified are the two under the Secondary School for Boys in Rabat; No. 3. in the front part of St. Paul's Catacombs compound; No. 23. under the Government nursery opposite St. Paul's Catacombs; and the three in the older Christian catacomb under St. Agatha's Church.

Secondary Boys School, Rabat: The original catacomb, located to the left below a short flight of stairs, has two rectangular, central rooms, behind the rear one of which are five chambers recessed within the walls. Each chamber contains a double tomb recessed in the wall on either side of a passageway and at the back of it. The layout of the first room is similar but smaller. In both rooms are benches made of stone blocks for mourners or those engaged in funeral rites. In addition, the slabs of stone for closing the entrances to the chambers are placed around the rooms. Each slab is about 4' high, $2\frac{1}{2}'$ wide and 6" thick, and is extended at the back by a plug of the same stone about 10" thick that just fits into the frame of the entrance to the chambers. Some of these stones are incised with an outline of a tool apparently being one of those used in the trade represented by the club. At the top, moreover, some of them bear an incision, diamond shaped in form, in the centre of which is a small aperture that extends to the back of the stone. The individual tombs have a flat floor about 6' long and 4' wide with a low rim 4" high at the outside edge; over the tomb is a recess 3' high with a three centred arch across it.

An extension of the original catacomb was constructed on the other side of a corridor extending below the same flight of stairs that serves the original catacomb. It has a rectangular entrance room some 9' wide and 12' long with bare walls. Beyond are several passageways on the sides of which are recessed a number of double trough-like tombs, and at the end of one passageway are several tombs with window-like entrances recessed within barrel vaulted niches. In the centre of the entrance room is a block of dressed stone measuring about 30" × 24" and about 16" high. It has a rim of the same stone around it about 3/4" high and $2\frac{1}{2}''$ wide except in the centre of one of the long sides where there is a space of about 5" without a rim. This stone apparently was an agape table and was either the first or more likely was made in a hurry to comply with a regulation laid down by the Church (see The Agape). Recessed behind in the corridor beyond this room is a proper agape table surrounded by a platform a recess 3' high with a three centred arch across it.

Catacomb No. 3: It was originally made up of four chambers containing tombs; three chambers were recessed off the end rectangular room and one off the passageway half way down. A large stone slab like those described above is beside each of the entrances to the four chambers, and the layout of the tombs in each is likewise similar.

An addition to the original catacomb was laid out on both sides of the passageway extending from the outside entrance. There are several passageways with tombs recessed in one side or both, and in two of these additional areas is an agape table with a semicircular platform around it recessed on the side of a passageway.

Of much interest in this catacomb is the slab used to close the frame of one of the chambers, and for making a libation through an aperture at the top extending down and through the back. The front surface of this slab contains fourteen

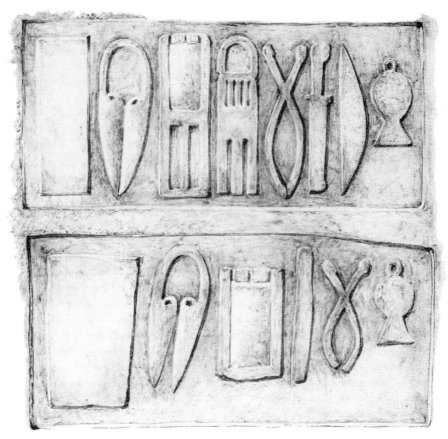

39. Medical Instruments II Century

diagrams depicting the instruments used by the physician and surgeon members of this funeral club (figure 39). These II century instruments have been identified from left to right in the top row and continuing in the same order in the second row as follows.[12]

1. Whetstone for sharpening knives and/or ointment slab.
2. Surgical shears or scissors.
3. Medical box; probably divided into compartments and of wood.
4. Vaginal speculum.
5. Surgical tongs or forceps or pincers.

[12] Dr. Paul Cassar, Balzan, Malta, "Surgical Instruments on a Slab in Roman Malta", Medical History, 1974, Welcome Institute for the History of Medicine, pp. 89 to 93.

6. Possibly a chisel with handle and flat blade for chopping bones, division of ribs, etc.
7. Possibly a bleeding bowl, side view.
8. Bleeding cup or cupping vessel.
9. Whetstone as no. 1.
10. Surgical shears or scissors as no. 2.
11. Portable ointment box.
12. Etui or portable probe case.
13. Surgical tongs, etc. as no. 5.
14. Possibly a bleeding bowl as no. 8.

Catacomb No. 23:   This was originally only an extended Punic tomb at the foot of a Punic shaft. The shaft was converted into a staircase and the usual slab with a plug at the back was placed in the frame of the tomb. The slab is now located in the adjoining room, leaning against the left wall.

A catacomb was later extended, probably in the latter part of the II century, from the same entrance by the excavation of a series of rooms and passageways. The entrance room on the right contains an agape table surrounded on three sides by a platform set within a semicircular wall on the right. There are several tombs with window-like entrances on either end of the wall and in the centre are the outlines of a group of tools incised in the wall which appear to have been those used by the fossors (figure 40). Beyond the entrance room are a number of tombs recessed within the walls on either side of the passageways.

St. Agatha's Church: The three funeral club catacombs in this older area under St. Agatha's Church were each originally formed with a chamber or two within which were two tombs recessed on either side of a passageway and two at the back. For each chamber there was the usual slab with a plug to close it. Some of these are still standing in front of the chamber entrances.

One of these catacombs, which had two chambers, each on one side of a corner of the wall, appears to have been altered to use the space in front to install an agape table and platform. As a result only a narrow space was left for a recessed passageway between the platform and the wall on the other side.

Subsequently, all three of these funeral club catacombs underwent a number of alterations due to the formation of a large catacomb surrounding all three completely with Christian type tombs and even converting one of their chambers into a passageway to a lower group of tombs.

9. *Ta' Mintna Catacombs:*   On a side street off a park at the crossing of two roads running from Mqabba to Qrendi there are three separate catacombs in a row. Each had a separate staircase that may have been extended from a Punic shaft but now only the entrance to the centre catacomb is open. The key to the iron gate may be obtained from the National Museum. These catacombs, which

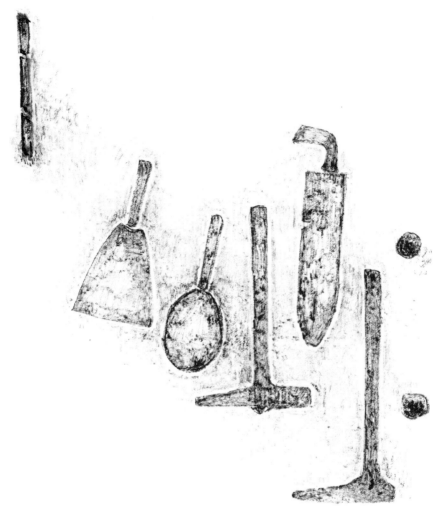

40. Tools for Excavating Catacombs II Century

essentially are very similar, are each composed of small oven like tombs, recessed in the walls on either side of passageways. They have window-like entrances recessed in barrel vaulted niches. In the rear wall of each is a Punic type stilted arch niche about 9″ × 9″ and 3″ deep on one side or both of which are small niches about 3″ wide, 5″ high and 2″ deep at the base but at the top where they come to a point it is flange with the surface of the wall. This might indicate that they were excavated during the II–III century.

The first of these three catacombs appears to have been that on the far right, and that several generations later the centre one was excavated. The latter has an agape table which is in exceptionally good condition. A peculiarity of this table is that the rim extends over the concave space above the floor which was intended for a vase. As a result, it would not have been possible to wash any particles of food through the small aperture below the rim, which would indicate that the table was intended to have milk or wine poured on it as a libation, although food could have been placed on it if it had been covered with a cloth.

The third catacomb, which was probably excavated a generation or two later, is notable for its beautiful shell headed niches over the window-like entrances to the tombs (figure 32).

In recent times these three catacombs have been connected by cutting through a tomb on each side of the centre catacomb. In the centre of the back of the catacomb on the right end, a well was cut into it from above and the whole catacomb may have been used as a cistern.

10. *Jewish Catacombs:* The Jewish origin of six catacombs in Rabat is evidenced in several ways: the first tombs were multiple in the traditional form; and in all these catacombs, the menorah appears in different places. It is interesting, however, to observe how these early Jews came to follow various forms and usages in conformity with local customs and habits: they constructed their catacombs in the same way and with the same kinds of tombs as was being done by the neo-Punics and later the Christians; they placed their catacombs in areas surrounded by those of the neo-Punics and Christians; and they developed them as the others did by using the shafts and tombs which had been used by the Punics before them.

Like the neo-Punics and Christians, the Jews placed various kinds of pottery in the tombs and they used Greek in denoting the names of those buried in the tombs. Likewise, the boat and the palm leaf are found on the walls of the Jewish tombs, just as on those of the Christians. And finally, as indicated by a seventh catacomb with Christian features, which is apparently an extension of one that was Jewish, some of them eventually were converted to Christianity.

As indicated by the sherds found in the tombs, the Jewish catacombs were among the first; one of the four original tombs is located in a catacomb under St. Agatha's Church, and the others are in catacombs No. 10, No. 12 and No. 13 respectively, which are under the Government nursery opposite St. Paul's Catacombs. The first and third are traditional in form and were intended for a number of bodies, i.e., 4 and 11 respectively, while the other two may have been remodelled from Punic tombs.

While the catacomb under St. Agatha's Church, No. 10, No. 12, and No. 13

were all extended from a single tomb, possibly up a century later, it appears that catacomb No. 14 under the Government nursery was conceived and constructed in the III century with the intent of being extended in three directions. An extension was begun to the right of the landing below the steps from the outside but it appears that it had to be abandoned as, when breaking through the wall at the end of the gallery, it was found that a II–III century catacomb was beyond it. An extension to the left of the landing, however, which is now identified as No. 17A, was completed, and this catacomb was subsequently extended by the construction of a catacomb now identified as No. 17B, which is located on the other side of the same landing below the stairs which is now used for catacomb No. 17A. As catacomb No. 17B contains three agape tables, a recognized feature of Christian catacombs from the II century onwards, it appears that it was constructed by Jews who had been converted, and whose forbears had used catacomb No. 17A and those connected with it, i.e., Nos. 12, 13, and 14, and possibly the other Jewish catacombs in the area as well.

The types of tombs in most Jewish catacombs seem to follow the same general progression as those in the Christian catacombs. However, a larger proportion of some early types continued to appear in their later catacombs than in the Christian. One of these is the original Punic type, either with only the square window-like entrance or that which came to be recessed within a barrel vaulted niche. Another is a combination of the primitive trough-like tomb, constructed in series of two to four, and the arcosolium which has a semi-circular arch extending lengthwise over them, hereafter identified as multiple arcosolium.

Catacomb under St. Agatha's Church: The original tomb in this catacomb is located in an open area on the right of the entrance corridor. The tomb is recessed behind the wall on the left. It has a window-like entrance about 4' above the floor, behind which is a rectangular room about 8' long, 5' 6" wide and 4' high. On the left side of the flat floor is a low bank with four headrests in it. The bodies lay in a row across the tomb without a partition wall between them. Incised in the outside wall above the entrance are some names in Greek, below which is a menorah.

The open area in front of the tomb was cut out apparently from around a Punic shaft; two Punic tombs, now blocked, can be seen high above. Surrounding the open area are six tombs behind window-like entrances recessed in barrel vaulted niches, some with short, fluted columns on either side of the entrance, and two loculi. A simple outline of a palm is incised in one of the walls. Another part of the catacomb, which is a continuation of the corridor extending from the entrance, contains two tombs with window-like entrances recessed within barrel vaulted niches, and two loculi.

Catacomb No. 12: The original tomb is located to the right of the landing below the stairs. A small, rectangular door opens into a passageway

157

between a rectangular recess on either side, each of which is 8' long, 5' 6" wide and 4' high. The one on the right has a low bank on the near side with five headrests in it, and that on the left has a bank with six headrests.

Outside, in the wall in front of the landing, a menorah (figure 30) with a three legged stand has been incised. To the left of the landing is a doorway to a room with two free-standing double canopy tombs, a Punic type tomb, three tombs with a window-like entrance recessed within a barrel vaulted niche, an arcosolium and two loculi. Above the floor by the right wall an arch has been cut out that leads to catacomb No: 13.

At the left end of the room, the floor drops 6", beyond which are two free standing tombs with window-like entrances recessed within barrel vaulted niches, three recessed tombs with window-like entrances recessed in barrel vaulted niches, two Punic type tombs and one loculus.

Catacomb No. 10: This is one of the most interesting small catacombs in Rabat. At the left of the landing below the stairs is a 20" square entrance with a menorah incised on its right side. Inside is the original tomb chamber of this catacomb, dating from the I–II century. The chamber is about 5' 6" long, 7' wide and 5' high. It is divided by a passageway; to the left there are three trough-like tombs with a low wall between them and on the right side is a single trough-like tomb behind which is a bank.

Straight on from the landing is a doorway, above which a menorah has been incised. Inside is a rectangular room some 9' wide and 12' long, in the left wall of which is a double arcosolium with a wall between the two tombs. Beyond this room is another rectangular room of about the same size, containing two multiple arcosoli, each covered with stone slabs cut into tiles.

Back in the first room is an entrance on its right with a large, stone door swinging on its own pivots, which opens into a room about 12' × 8'. On either side is a stone bench. Recessed in the wall on each side are two trough-like tombs, the rear one of which is covered with a double-pitched slab like a saddleback tomb.

Catacomb No. 13: This is an exceptionally large catacomb containing: a small gallery to the right with the original tomb; a small room straight ahead; a medium size room beyond; a large room running off to the left of the latter; and to the left of the landing a large room with a gallery extending from it on the left.

The original tomb at the back of the gallery on the right is a small, oven-like Punic type with a window-like entrance 20' square. On the right side of the gallery is a double arcosolium with a dividing wall between the two troughs. On the left is a full length loculus.

The entrance to the small room ahead of the landing has a menorah above it. The room contains a trough-like tomb on either side of the passageway and a tomb in the floor. A screen wall at the end of the room has a square window on either side of the doorway to the next room.

To the right of the passageway in this medium size room is a free standing double canopy tomb with a curb on two sides. The walls beside a narrow passageway around three sides of the canopy tomb contain three arcosoli and three loculi tombs.

In the large room to the left are two free standing canopy tombs, one double and one triple, both with dividing walls. In the surrounding walls are two single and three multiple arcosoli and three loculi tombs. In the rear wall of this room, a hole has been cut above a tomb on either side, which leads to catacomb 17A.

In the room to the left of the landing below the outside entrance is a double canopy tomb with a dividing wall. Recessed in the wall beyond and that on the right are two single and two multiple arcosoli with dividing wall, and two loculi. In back of the canopy tomb is a small passageway behind which is double arcosolium tomb.

On either side of the gallery to the left of the above room are one single, three double and five multiple arcosoli with dividing walls, and one tomb with a window-like entrance recessed within a barrel vaulted niche. In the double arcosolium at the end on the right of the gallery is a beautiful menorah carved into the centre of its head. At the end of the gallery is a low arch extending from the floor to connect this catacomb with catacomb No. 12.

Catacomb No. 14: To the right of the landing below the outside entrance is a short gallery with three double arcosoli with dividing walls. At the back is a hole in the wall on the other side of which is a destroyed catacomb dating from the II–III century.

Straight on from the landing is an arched doorway over which a menorah is incised. The room beyond contains on the left a single arcosolium with a loculus behind, and a multiple arcosolium with dividing walls, behind which is also a loculus tomb, and two tombs in the floor covered with large slabs each 20″ × 26″, and on the right are two multiple arcosoli.

The room beyond contains a free standing, large double canopy tomb with a dividing wall, which has a curb around all its sides into which small tombs have been cut (figure 35). In the left side of this tomb are incised a diagram of a boat and a name written in Greek above it (figure 31). In the walls beside a narrow passageway are four multiple arcosoli with dividing walls, two tombs with a window-like entrance recessed within a barrel vaulted niche, and three loculi. The two tombs at the left, rear corner have drains cut through into the back wall.

To the left at the rear corner is a room about 9′ × 12′ without tombs which presumably was intended for holding funeral rites.

Catacomb No. 17A: To the left of the landing below the outside entrance of catacomb No. 14, is a passageway that leads to this catacomb. On its left is a bank recessed in the wall which may have served to hold a corpse before placing it in a tomb. On the right is a double arcosolium with a dividing wall.

In the room beyond is a free standing canopy tomb with only one section recessed in it, and to its left are three double canopy tombs with dividing walls. Recessed in the walls are one single and two double arcosoli, one of which has a dividing wall, and four oven-like tombs with window-like entrances recessed within barrel vaulted niches. The stairs lead to catacomb No. 17B.

Catacomb No. 17B: This catacomb may be entered from the outside directly as well as through catacomb No. 17A. As evidenced by the agape table in the small room on the left and the pair of agape tables dividing the room beyond, this catacomb was typically Christian. If the openings, which have been noted in the walls, connecting catacomb No. 12 with No. 13 and No. 13 with No. 17A, were made in order to enter catacomb No. 17B, as they suggest, it might be assumed that the Jews, who had been converted to Christianity, found it necessary to pretend they were only entering a Jewish catacomb in order to avoid possible persecution by the Roman authorities. Accordingly, it would appear that catacomb 17B had been constructed some years before 313 when Christianity became tolerated. In that event, the stairway entrance from the outside would not have been opened until after that time.

To the left of the small room with the agape table is a gallery with a single and three multiple arcosoli with dividing walls; opposite the small room to the right is a narrow gallery with a few loculi.

Surrounding the pair of agape tables in the room beyond are seven loculi, and in the wall beyond are three openings into the next room. The latter room contains three free standing canopy tombs, one of which has a dividing wall. A peculiarity of some of these canopy tombs is that the openings above the long sides are rectangular rather than a semicircular arch. Recessed in the walls are five double arcosoli each with a dividing wall.

In the end room, there are three double canopy tombs, one of which has a dividing wall. Recessed in the walls are three double arcosoli, one of which has a dividing wall, an open bank and two loculi. The gallery, which extends out from the room but never completed might indicate this was the last catacomb to be excavated by those of Jewish origin.

11. *St. Catald's Church Catacomb:* This small catacomb is below a church which may be one of a number which succeeded an original chapel built about 400. It is diagonally opposite the parish Church of St. Paul beside which is St. Paul's grotto.

Typical of the catacombs built in the late II to III century, it was extended from a neo-Punic shaft/tomb, both of which are still to be seen behind the right side of the agape table platform. In front of the agape table is a passageway running through the middle of the catacomb. On either side are canopy tombs, one placed next to the other, and there are several on the other side of a passageway across the end of the catacomb.

The floors of these tombs are fitted with drains, recessed on either side of the centre rib, and a low bank at one end with two headrests on either side of which is a small hole for supporting a short vase or amphora.

12. St. Paul's Catacombs: These are the most representative of the large catacombs as regards their growth and alteration. They began with family catacombs cut out around Punic shafts and tombs, one with trough-like tombs and another with loculi. Subsequently, a number of catacombs were excavated at what is now an intermediary level, in one of which a funeral chapel appears to have been installed with an agape table and platform, subsequently destroyed (figure 24). Following this, the central part of the catacombs was constructed. It is now above both sides of the two large crypts which were later cut out by clearing away some of the tombs and installing two large agape tables with platforms on the right crypt and an altar area on the left. During the period of severe persecutions, which extended over most of 250–306, tunnels were cut into the sides of the catacombs. One was from catacomb no. 3, which is located just in front of the main catacomb (as that catacomb was one recognized as belonging to a funeral club, permitted by the Roman authorities, it could be entered without interference). The other tunnel was constructed from the street at the rear, brought underneath the garden and through a series of tombs at the back behind the crypt at the left. With all these changes and alterations causing some parts to be destroyed or eliminated and others abandoned, St. Paul's Catacombs now present a strange and neglected appearance like some old village that has never been modernized.

These extensive catacombs, some parts of which have been blocked recently, were 220 feet at their widest axis, which runs N/W and S/E, and the East-West axis was 150 feet. The combined length of the gallaries was 2,750 feet and the total area covered 2,590 square yards. The average depth of the catacombs is 15 feet, the lowest being 18 feet which was necessary in view of the older tombs cut in the area above. There are an estimated 900 tombs remaining in all while 500 were destroyed. As no large pits for the internment of the poor were found, it is assumed the catacombs were for wealthier families. All of the tombs had been vandalized and all but one in which bones have been replaced, are empty.[13]

The most remarkable parts of St. Paul's Catacombs are the twin crypts at the

[13] A. A. Caruana, "Ancient Pagan Tombs and Christian Cemeteries", 1898.

foot of the stairs leading down from the entrance on Hal Bajjada Street. These crypts, hewn in the living rock, may date from the IV century. The entrance from the street may have been enlarged in the middle of the IV century when it was no longer necessary to secret the catacomb.

Entering the two large crypts at the foot of the steps, which is like coming into a vaulted cathedral, a large pillar stands in front dividing them. Looking to the right and to the left, one is amazed at this subterranean beauty. The sides and roof, worn with age, are aglow with blue and green, like a grotto, and the crypts, with recessed tombs surrounding them and containing inexplicable forms and shapes cut in the live rock of the floors, are like stepping into a weird world of the ancient past, which they are.

The crypt on the right is 40 feet in length, 16 feet wide and 10 feet high. It is identified as a longitudinal nave. At each end is a raised platform, 16 by 18 feet, in the centre of which with its edge directly above the end of the floor, is a circular area 4 feet and 4 inches in diameter. It has a raised edge around it about 2 inches high, except at the front a crescent is cut out down to the floor. These circular areas are agape tables (figure 23) used for funeral rites of early Christians (see section on The Agape).

The crypt on the left of the column is about 30 feet long, 12 feet wide and 12 feet high. It is considered to represent a crossnave. There are two steps across its front. Above is a large rectangular recess which may have been used to receive the altar on which the holy sacrifice was placed.

Making a hairpin turn to the right at the foot of the stairs and following a narrow passageway to the right of the agape table and platform and continuing between several tombs, some steps will be seen leading to an intermediate area through a door. Within this area there appears to have been a funeral chapel (figure 24) surrounded by several groups of tombs dating apparently from the II–III centuries.

To the left of this room is a narrow passageway which may be closed but those interested may, if they come prepared with a torch, ask one of the guides to accompany them. Passing through a narrow passageway and past where a Punic shaft and tomb had been, it comes to some steps. Going down and around a tomb in the floor on the right, and then continuing down a passageway, two or three stones will be seen on the right forming steps leading up through a broken floor of a trough-like tomb. Coming out of that tomb, it is necessary to climb over three more trough-like tombs to reach an open area. On the left is a hole in the wall through which one can enter another room with tombs which has a skylight beyond. Both of these small catacombs apparently date from the II century. To return to the crypt, look for the entrance through the fourth tomb on the right in the inner chamber!

On entering the crypt again, turn to the right and enter the next passageway down a few steps on the right to two large tombs on the left. The first is a saddle-back with Roman type corners and the second is similar but with a flat roof. They are so large and grand, they might have been for some converted Roman officials in the IV century.

Returning to the corridor and proceeding to the last gallery on the right that extends through to the end of the catacomb, dating from the III century apparently, there are a number of double canopy tombs on the left side. At the far corner of the third cross corridor on the left is what remains of an inscription bearing the word EVTYXION. Half way along on the right side, some tombs can be seen above through the broken wall, which date apparently from the II–III centuries. Near the end of the gallery is a large open space on both sides, which may have been an alcove for one or two families; looking back and up on the left side, the blocked entrance to another catacomb in the intermediary level can be seen which probably dates from the II–III centuries.

At the end of the gallery and in the cross corridor on the left are two saddle-back tombs, and at the end is the only tomb in these catacombs with a window-like entrance, recessed in a barrel vaulted niche.

Coming back and crossing over to the gallery on the right, and stepping down into the back of the crypt, the remains of some frescos can be seen on the left wall.

Turning right between the two agape tables and passing by the foot of the stairs and across the end of the next crypt, a narrow passageway will be found that leads to the right and up to a tunnel through a number of tombs, which was constructed probably in the middle of the III century when the persecutions made it necessary to close the catacombs otherwise and enter them without detection.

On the left, before reaching the approach to the tunnel, is a flight of crude steps with a railing; it leads to a large double area filled with loculi tombs. At the right end is an iron gate to the garden, the entrance from which was formed by a former Punic shaft. In the left end, was once a cistern cut through the surface and a bit into the floor, when this II century catacomb was used as a cistern.

13. *St. Agatha's Church Catacombs:* St. Agatha's Church, which is off a lane to the right of Hal Bajjada Street, a few feet up the road from St. Paul's Catacombs, contains three main groups of tombs. One of these, a Jewish catacomb, is beside a courtyard, and is not usually open to the public. The other two are entered by stairs below the front of the Church. The carved blocks inserted above in the facade of the Church are particularly well done and interesting. The stairs lead to a crypt, a former cave, which is 37 feet long and 12 feet wide. It is of special interest as it contains thirty 15th century life size frescos, which were partially restored in 1881. They are mostly of St. Agatha, and, in addition, there is one of the Madonna holding the Child with the globe, and some of saints, among whom are St. Leonard holding a chain, symbolic of his charity toward captives when he was a courtier of a king in the sixth century, St. Anthony bearing a cross consecrating the crypt, St. Margherite holding a rope to which a dragon is tied, St. Blase who was martyred in 315, St. Lucia beheaded in 303, and St. Venera a martyr from Marseilles who came to Malta during the persecution of the Christians. [14]

According to the tradition commemorated in this crypt, a Christian girl of a leading family in Catania, took refuge in the cave in 249–250 (when it appears three funeral club catacombs and probably the large extension around them, which are directly to the rear of the cave, were already existing). She had promised Quintianus, the prefect of Catania, that she would marry him after completing a veil she was weaving. However, like Penelope, St. Agatha, during her stay in the cave, would undo at night all that she had woven during the day. When finally she returned to Catania and still rejected Quintianus, he had her breasts removed and she died a martyr. [14]

The three funeral club catacombs directly behind the crypt and the II–III century large catacomb extending from them are not usually open to the public, but the III century addition on the right is. A passageway, which has been cut out in recent years, leads to it. This large catacomb, containing several hundred tombs, appears to have originated with a Punic shaft and a large tomb 13 feet below it. It was subsequently extended on a systematic plan by passageways in all four directions from it with tombs on either side.

Most of these tombs are of an intricate design, i.e., 1. canopy double tombs, which are within four walls opening into arches above on three sides, and were sealed with slabs placed lengthwise over the individual tombs (figure 35); 2. saddleback double tombs, which are likewise within four walls of which three open to arches on the sides above but are closed on top of the individual tombs with a stone cut to resembly a small house, and have a small opening on the side below into which the bodies could be inserted and then sealed (figure 36); and 3. oven-like tombs, recessed into walls behind a square or rectangular entrance, within a barrel vaulted arch, or with a half dome arch above, some of which have been cut out in the shape of a shell headed niche (figure 32).

On the side of one of these tombs, a small monogram of Christ has been incised (figure 29), and on the side of the wall at the head of one tomb is an inscription in Greek within a decorated framework. There are also two very fine and well preserved frescos on the side of two tombs; one is of a circular floral arrangement with a wreath and ribbons flowing from it, and the other is of a peacock with its tail spread upward.

[14] A. A. Caruana, "The Crypt of St. Agatha's in Hal Bajjada District", 1899.

A part of this catacomb is lighted but part is not, which may be seen, however, if accompanied by a guide, and preferably also equipped with a strong electric torch.

SHRINES

There are several shrines still to be seen which apparently were used by early Christians. One is to the right of St. Paul's Church in Rabat below a small building constructed over steps leading down to where there had been a deep cave beside the ditch of Roman Melita. According to tradition, a shrine had been established there in the III century. Round plaques on the walls on either side of the staircase, representing St. Peter and St. Paul, which have been identified as Byzantine, testify to the fact that this had been a holy place since at least the VIII century when the Church of Malta was placed under Constantinople.

Another Christian shrine, apparently, was in a cave at Wied Hanzir, probably also in the III century when the severe persecutions made it necessary to hide them in order to avoid detection. Both sides of this cave are covered with crosses of the crucifix blotting out inscriptions which were apparently in Greek.

When Theodoseus I., who reigned from 379–395, made Christianity the official state religion of the Roman Empire, and issued an edict cancelling the right of ownership of Pagans to their religious sites, it appears the Church took possession of the country house at Burmarrad (see Country Estates) believed to have been identified with the shipwreck of St. Paul in 56 (60).

According to Acts 28, Publius, the chief magistrate of Malta, who had lands in the neighbourhood of the bay where the shipwreck took place, took St. Paul and St. Luke in and entertained them hospitably for three days. It so happened that Publius' father was in bed suffering from recurrent bouts of fever and dysentry. St. Paul visited him and, after prayer, laid his hands upon him and healed him; whereupon the other sick people on the island came also and were cured.

Constructed over a room of the villa, which apparently was claimed especially by the Christians in the IV century, stands today a small church dedicated to St. Paul. It replaced one still standing, which had replaced one built in the XIII or XIV century that stood on the Punic/Roman ruins of the room.

These churches indicate that this room, built during the time of Augustus (27 B.C.–14 A.D.), where there was a cistern with a marble lid and supporting bases of marble for the amphorae and a base of an trapeza, may have been the one in which St. Paul performed his miracles of healing. This was the front room of the house proper and thus, receiving the sick there, would not have interfered with the life of the household. According to tradition, moreover, St. Paul baptised some of the converts in that room as well. This room was progressively set off from the remainder of the house and acquired a separate entrance and exit, as if it had been a shrine where early Christians came to pay homage.

The significance of this room is indicated, moreover, by the relics found there recalling the shipwreck of St. Paul and himself, and the fact that three successive churches were built over it, all of which were dedicated to St. Paul Milqi meaning "he who was met". As stated by the Italian excavators (1963–68), "this room is, therefore, one of the most important monuments of Maltese historical tradition".

Near this room, a small stone block was found showing St. Paul and a ship run aground. This block of calcareous stone, which is extremely friable and arenacious from the sedimentation of the sea, is identified with the small island of Selmunette where St. Paul's shipwreck is believed to have occurred. It has a fairly regular cross hatched design on three surfaces, above which are other engravings of which two represent a ship and another a human figure. One of these ships has a Latin sail and an oar-like rudder (Acts 27 states they "lashed the steering paddles"), run aground on a rock under the keel at the prow (Acts 27 states "the bow stuck fast and remained immovable, while the stern was being pounded to pieces by the breakers"). The figure clearly belongs to the tradition of iconography of St. Paul existing in the IV century. It is vigorously engraved and is of a bald man with a pointed beard, leaning on a cane having the shape of a tare. Wearing a Roman tunic and carrying such a cane, the figure was typically of a monk of an Egyptian monastery of the Vth century on and could well have been made by such a monk as a votive to St. Paul during the latter half of the VII or the first score of the VIII century.

There is an inscription in Greek letters, spelling in Latin, Paulus, on one of the blocks which formed a boundary of the house. It is now set into the wall between the apse of the church built in Medieval times, which is cut through by the foundations of the present church, and the threshold of the former chapel placed much below the level of the existing church.[15]

BASILICAS

In addition to the chapels built by the Church beside several of the more important catacombs, and the funeral chapels, such as that in St. Paul's Catacombs (figure 24), the Church, in about the middle of the IV century, seems to have converted the two crypts in St. Paul's Catacombs into a cemeterial Basilica in which the native Christian congregation with its priests and presbyters assembled for the celebration of holy mass, etc. The crypt on the left is said most likely to have been the men's division who, according to custom, were shown in by the clerics, while that on the right was for the women who were escorted by

---

[15] "Missione Archeologica a Malta", Vols. 63–8.

the deaconesses. The whole place was embellished with holy scenes and pictures of the martyrs identified particularly with Malta.

According to the excavations made by the Missione Archeologica of Malta between 1963 and 1970, it appears that in the IV to V century, the Christians took over the Copper Age temple at Tas Silg, or what remained of it after the abandonment of the Punic/Roman sanctuary in the I century. The Italian excavators found that at the beginning of the V century or just before, there was a sudden, multiple building of architectural structures, which remained until an Arab mosque was built in the IX century. Oil lamps with Christian emblems, a cross on a column, etc., testified that there was a Christian monastery and settlement at Tas Silg.

Evidence was found that while the Byzantine structures were generally small and somewhat carelessly built with stones taken from other structures, there was evidence of the richness of the monastery and the church. An entrance in the west wall of the Copper Age temple had been made for the monastery, and its inside construction had been rearranged to provide for a rectangular baptismal basin with two steps leading down on either end. In the centre of the apse, just barely protruding from the alignment of the end wall, was the altar, consisting of a table supported by a central pillar, embedded in the ancient cement floor. In the IX century, Byzantine fortifications were built, which, apparently, repulsed the first attack of the Arabs in 837,[16] but in 870 the Arabs successfully occupied Malta.

Within the courtyard of L'Abbatija tad-Dejr catacombs are a number of old building stones, including a capital and a part of a column as well as traces of post-Roman polychrome floor mosaic that may have formed part of a basilica.

[16] "Missione Archeologica a Malta", Vols. 63–70.

SELECTED BIBLIOGRAPHY

A. G. Agius, "Ghar Dalam Cave", 1970.

Thomas H. Ashby, "Roman Malta", 1915.

Eric Becker, "Malta Sotterranea: Studien zur altchristlichen und judischen Sepulkralkunst", Strassburg, 1913.

Mgr. Arthur Bonnici, "History of the Church of Malta", Vol. I, 1967.

Vincenzo Borg/Benedetto Rocco "L'Ipogeo di Tac-Caghki a Malta", 1972.

L. Bernabo Brea, "Sicily", 1966.

A. A. Caruana, "Ancient Pagan Tombs and Christian Cemeteries", 1898.

A. A. Caruana, "Report on the Phoenician and Roman Antiquities", 1882.

A. A. Caruana, "Recent Discoveries at Notabile", 1881.

A. A. Caruana, "The Crypt of St. Agatha's in Hal Bajjada District", 1889.

J. D. Evans, "The Prehistoric Antiquities of the Maltese Islands", 1971.

J. D. Evans, "Malta in Antiquity, Blue Guide, Malta", 1968.

S. Gsell, "Histoire Ancienne L'Afrique", Vol. IV.

Margaret Guido, "Sicily: An Archaeological Guide", 1967.

J. Lempriere, "Classical Dictionary", 1958.

E. R. Leopardi, "Malta's Heritage", 1969.

G. R. Levy, "Gate of Horn", 1946.

Livy, "The War with Hannibal", Book XXI.

A. Mayr, "Die Insel Malta in altertum", 1909.

"Medical History", 1974, Medical Institute of the History of Medicine, London.

Sabatino Moscati, "The World of the Phoenicians", 1968.

Susan Raven, "Rome in Africa", 1969.

"Reports on the Working of the Museum of Malta", 1909–10; February 1929; 1929–35; 1965.

D. H. Trump, "Skorba", 1966.

D. H. Trump, "Malta: An Archaeological Guide", 1972.

Universita degli Studi di Roma/Consiglio Nazionale delle Ricerche, "Missione Archeologica a Malta", 1963, 4, 5, 6, 7, 9, 1970.